MW01203888

AUTOMOTIVE TROUBLE SHOOTING
For WW2 Wheeled Vehicles

Volume 1

Edited by Robert V. Notman

This book is dedicated to those unsung heroes of world war two—the mechanics and drivers. Without their dedication and duty to their machines the troops on the line would not have been the best equipped army in the field.

Published by Robert V. Notman
Tallahassee, Florida USA

Copyright © 2005 by Robert V. Notman
ALL RIGHTS RESERVED
First Edition

No part of this book may be reproduced in any form, in an electronic retrieval system or otherwise, without the prior written permission of the copyright owner. Contact: notmanr7@comcast.net

Printed in the United States of America.

Other Copyright or Trademarks Notices: All trademarks and copyright marks belong to their respective owners, lack of trademark or copyright indicator is in no way meant to detract from their owners right of ownership or use. Manufacturers or vendors listed here do not indicate endorsement of any kind by those manufacturers or vendors.   Pictures credited as noted.

Disclaimers: Some of the information posted here was correct for the day but has since been supplanted because of modern safety concerns.   If you choose to use any of the information you do so at your own risk. Please try to use common sense and be careful!

AUTOMOTIVE TROUBLE SHOOTING
For WW2 Wheeled Vehicles

Table of Contents

AUTOMOTIVE TROUBLE SHOOTING
For WW2 Wheeled Vehicles

CHAPTER 1

INTRODUCTION

1. PURPOSE.

This text was originally published for use in courses at The Ordnance School. Today, some sixty years later much of this information is style very useful. The beginner will find it helpful in trouble shooting the WW2 vehicle and even the experienced mechanic might learn a thing or three!

If you think about the scope of the war, it is hard to come to terms in sheer numbers. Have you every wondered why your 2 1/2-ton GMC truck is still here today? Could it be because there were some many of them? According to government records there were eleven types of 2 1/2-ton, 6x6 trucks. There were 676,433 purchased from July 1, 1940 through December 31, 1945. The same holds true for the various

categories of vehicles. In the light truck category there were 634,569 jeeps; 12,774 amphibious jeeps; and 248,634 3/4, 4x4 (6 types) trucks.

To put this in perspective, let's look at some other "items" that were procured during the war:
1/4-ton, trailers—143,371
Rifles, Garand .30 cal—4,014,731
Carbine, .30 cal—6,117,827
Helmets, M1—22,756,000
.30 cal cart. —25,065,834,000 rds
.45 cal cart.—4,072,000,000 rds
Cotton, Khaki shirts—72,869,000
Cotton, Khaki pants—71,125,000

What has any of this to do with trouble shooting WW2 vehicles?
Well, nothing really but I'm trying to impress upon you how it is that you still have a vehicle to work on...or

curse at as the case may be. Hopefully, this little book will help you figure out what's wrong with your truck. If there's nothing wrong with your truck, that's great...it's only a matter of time....so be prepared.

It should also be noted that some items suggested for use are no longer considered safe. The reader should use common sense and safe practices, such as, wearing eye and ear protection. The editor accepts no responsibility for the work you choose to do.

2. SCOPE.

This text outlines the general procedure for trouble shooting, repair, and adjustment of wheeled vehicles equipped with gasoline engines. It does not contain any general information on the construction or operation of the various units, and presumes that the student has a thorough understanding of automotive theory. This text is not a substitute for the manuals, for example, TM 9-803, TM 9-1803A and TM 9-1803B for the Willys MB and Ford GPW. Similar manuals are available for other WW2 military vehicles.

3. GENERAL.

a. Trouble shooting is the process of locating a malfunction by the elimination of possible causes in the order of their probability. Without a planned approach you can spend hours searching for a loose wire; with a systematic diagnosis the trouble can generally be located in a few minutes.

b. The systematic steps to take in trouble shooting are outlined in chapter 2. Cross references in this section refer to the paragraph in the following chapters which tells how to correct the fault once it is located.

c. Regularly scheduled tune up and adjustment will prolong the life of a vehicle and reduce the chance of breakdowns. The detailed instructions in chapters 3 to 8 may be used for this purpose.

d. All test methods have been simplified where possible to avoid special tools and elaborate equipment. Acceptable field expedients are included in some instances.

CHAPTER 2

ENGINE TROUBLE SHOOTING

4. GENERAL.

This chapter outlines general procedures for basic trouble shooting. The specific procedures for individual systems are given in detail in subsequent chapters.

5. CRANKING MOTOR WILL NOT CRANK ENGINE.

If the cranking motor will not crank the engine or does so slowly, the fault may be in the battery or the cranking motor. Check the battery first (par 12). Loose or broken battery or ground cables will cause cranking-motor failure. Clean the terminals, and tighten or replace the cables (par 13) if necessary. The contact terminal of the cranking-motor switch sometimes becomes corroded or burned and prevents a good contact. Check for this condition, and replace the switch if necessary. If the cranking motor does not operate after the above corrections have been made, it must be replaced (par 30).

6. ENGINE FAILS TO START.

a. General. When the engine , fails to start, the most probable cause is failure of the ignition system; the next most probable cause is trouble in , the fuel system. The spark test is one of the quickest ways to determine which of these two systems is responsible.

b. Spark test. Disconnect one wire from the spark plug With the ignition switch on and the cranking motor cranking the engine, hold the free end of the wire about 1/8 in. away from the engine block. If there is no, spark, the trouble is in the ignition system. If there is a spark, the trouble is probably in the fuel system.

c. No spark. Use the ammeter in diagnosing this condition. Normally the ammeter will show a slight discharge, the needle oscillating between 2 and 4 amperes. The following procedures should be followed for various ammeter readings:

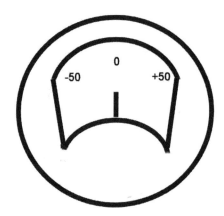

[1] Ammeter shows no discharge. A zero reading on the ammeter, with ignition turned on and the cranking motor cranking the engine, indicates that no current is flowing in the ignition primary circuit; therefore the following checks should be made on the units of the primary circuit:

(a) Make sure that the ignition .switch is fully turned on and that wiring connections are clean and tight.

(b) Turn on headlights to ascertain that current is flowing through ammeter. If ammeter does not show discharge, turn off headlight switch. Then disconnect wire at battery side of ammeter and make flash test to determine if current is flowing to the ammeter. Check and tighten con-

nections in circuit between cranking motor and ignition switch.
 (c) Remove distributor cap and check condition of points and point opening (par 21). Adjust or replace points as necessary.

(d) Check the continuity of circuit through the primary wire from ignition switch to coil and from coil to distributor. If current flows through the primary wire from switch to coil but not from coil to distributor, replace the coil (par 22). If curren1 flows through the primary wire to the distributor, the trouble is in the distributor (par 19, 20, 21).

(e) Check the continuity of circuit from ammeter to ignition switch, then through the ignition switch with switch turned on. Replace the wiring or switch as necessary (par 23).

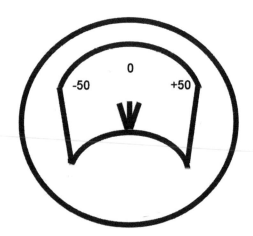

[2] Ammeter shows normal oscillating discharge. If the ammeter oscillates between 2 and 4 amperes' discharge with ignition turned on and the cranking motor cranking the engine, the primary circuit is functioning correctly. Trace the secondary circuit in the following manner:

(a) Remove the coil-to-distributor high-tension wire from distributor cap. Hold the end of the wire .about 3/8 .in. from a ground. With the cranking motor cranking the engine, note the spark. If a hot, snappy spark results, reinsert wire in distributor cap and proceed to (b). If a weak spark results, replace the condenser (par 20) in the distributor. If a weak spark persists, replace the coil (par 22). If no spark results, check high -tension wire from coil to distributor for continuity of circuit.

(b) With the high-tension wire from coil to distributor inserted in the distributor cap, remove the oap. Willi the cranking motor cranking the engine, observe the inside of the cap for visible current leaks (par 19).

(c) Check the condition of the distributor-cap center electrode by holding one end of a high-tension wire on the electrode and the other end about 3/8 in. from a ground. Crank engine with cranking motor. A spark should jump the gap from the high tension wire to ground. If no spark is produced, replace the cap (par 19).

(d) Remove the high-tension wire from coil to distributor at the distributor cap. Hold the end of high tension wire about 3/8 in. from the rotor. Crank engine and watch for spark. If a spark occurs, the rotor is defective (par 19).

(e) After determining that secondary current arrives at spark-plug wires, test each spark-plug wire for continuity of circuit (par 18). Replace wires which do not test correctly.

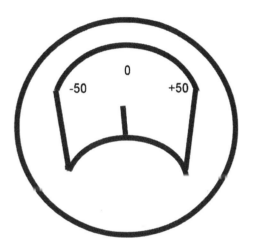

[3] Ammeter shows constant normal discharge. A constant discharge of 2 to 4 amperes indicates that the primary circuit is not being interrupted. Check in the following sequence:

(a) Disconnect the primary wire from coil to distributor at the distributor. If ammeter drops to 0, proceed to (b). If ammeter does not

drop to 0, reconnect wire at distributor and disconnect at coil. If ammeter then drops to 0, the wire is defective and must be replaced. If ammeter does not drop to 0, the coil is defective and must be replaced.
(b) Check distributor points, and adjust or replace if necessary (par 21).

(c) Check the insulation on the movable point and on the distributor primary terminal. Replace points or distributor as necessary.

(d) Disconnect condenser pigtail. Make flash test between pigtail terminal and distributor primary-wire terminal. If a flash occurs, replace condenser (par 20).

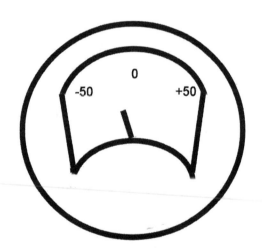

[4] Ammeter shows abnormal discharge with switch on. If the ammeter shows a discharge of over 4 amperes with the ignition switch on and with the switch off, the trouble lies beyond the ignition switch

and ahead of the primary exit at the coil. Test as follows:

(a) With ignition switch on, disconnect wire at the dead side of the switch. If the ammeter returns to 0, the switch is correct. If the ammeter does not return to 0, the switch is defective. Replace with one known to be good.

(b) With the switch known to be functioning properly, disconnect wire at primary entrance of coil. If the ammeter returns to 0, check terminal of coil for a grounded condition. If the terminal is not grounded, replace the coil. If the terminal is grounded, correct the grounded condition or replace the coil (par 22).

(c) If the ammeter still shows abnormal discharge after the primary wire is disconnected at the coil, replace wire from switch to coil.

[5] Ammeter shows abnormal discharge with switch either on or off. If an abnormal discharge exists whether the ignition switch is on or off, the trouble lies between the ammeter and the ignition switch. Shorts may also exist in the lighting circuit (between ammeter and light switch) or in the generator circuit. Test as follows:

(a) Remove wires from the discharge side of \he ammeter. The

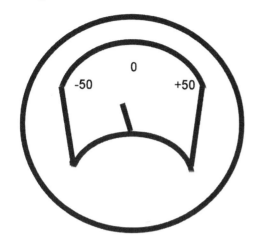

ammeter should then return to 0. With the lights off, touch the ammeter terminal with the terminal of the light circuit wire. If the ammeter shows a discharge, trace for a short in the wire from the ammeter to the light switch. If no short is present, check the generator circuit (par 25). If the generator circuit does not cause dischargo, the trouble lies either in the ignition switch or in the wire from the ammeter to the ignition switch.

(b) With ammeter-to-switch wire disconnected at both ends, connect a jumper lead between the ammeter terminal and the ignition-switch terminal. If the discharge still shows, replace the ignition switch. If the ammeter returns to 0, replace the ammeter-to-ignition-switch wire.

d. Weak spark at plugs.

[1] This condition may be caused by a weak battery. Check the battery, and charge or replace it if necessary (par 12).

[2] Remove the distributor cap and check condition of points. Clean and adjust, or replace if necessary (par 21).

[3] Check the condition of the rotor and cap. Replace the cap if the electrodes are burned, or the rotor if the segment is burned. Make sure the wires are dry and fully seated in the sockets of the distributor cap (par 19).

[4] Check condenser for short, and replace if necessary (par 20).

[5] Check all connections in the circuit from the cranking motor to the distributor. Clean and tighten as necessary (par 23).

[6] Check condition of high tension wires. Replace if wet, cracked, or swollen (par 18).

[7] If steps (1) through (6) do not eliminate the trouble, replace the ignition coil (par 22).

e. Good spark at plugs. If the engine will not start when the spark at the plugs is good, make sure first of all that the fuel tank is not empty and then proceed as follows:

7

[1] Check to see if gasoline is reaching the carburetor. Remove the air cleaner. While looking into the throat of the carburetor, work the throttle by hand. A spurt of gas should be visible. If it is, the trouble maybe water in the carburetor or a flooded engine.

[2] If no spurt of gas is seen, disconnect the fuel line at the carburetor. Work the hand operating lever on the fuel pump, and watch the end of the line. If there is no spurt of gasoline, the trouble maybe the fuel pump or a clogged line. If the spurt does occur, the carburetor is clogged up or the float valve is stuck closed.

7. **ENGINE RUNS BUT OPERATES IMPROPERLY**.

a. Continuous misfiring. The most likely source of trouble is the spark plugs, but a second possibility is low compression. Check as follows:

[1] First determine that the current is flowing to each plug; remove the plugs and check for dirty electrodes. Clean and adjust spark gap,

or replace the plugs as necessary (par 17).

[2] Inspect high tension wires. Replace them if wet or if their insulation is swollen or has deteriorated (par 18).

[3] Remove the distributor cap and check for burned electrodes or cracks. Replace cap if defective (par 19).

[4] Conditions contributing to low compression will also cause misfiring in one or more cylinders. If the remedies given above do not correct the trouble, check the compression of all cylinders (par 9) and make whatever repairs are necessary.

b. Erratic misfiring at idling speeds.
[1] Check the operation of the choke mechanism (par 55, 56). One of the most common causes of misfiring at idling speeds is incorrect carburetor - idling adjustment (par 57) or incorrect float-level ad-

justment (par 53). Make adjustments as required.

[2] Check ignition-system units, starting with the spark plugs, until all ignition-system faults are corrected or eliminated.

[3] Check for vacuum leaks at windshield-wiper hose, intake manifold gasket, vacuum lines, and carburetor. Check the possibility of water entering the cylinder due to a leaking cylinder -head gasket, a cracked block, or a loose head bolt.

[4} If the condition still exists, check valve clearance and valve mechanism operation (par 212); perform engine compression test (par 9); and make necessary adjustments and repairs.

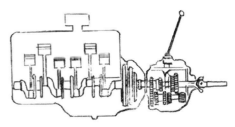

c. Misfiring at high speeds or under full load. Misfiring at high speeds or under full load is commonly caused by a weak secondary current in the ignition circuit or a lean carburetor mixture. However, weak valve springs are another cause.

[1] Remove spark plugs and make sure they are the correct type. Clean them and adjust the gap (par 17). Make sure the gap is the same as called for in engine specifications.

[2] Remove the distributor cap; check the point opening and test the spring tension (par 21). Adjust point opening and spring tension, or replace points as necessary.

[3] A weakened coil caused by shorting out of secondary winding will cause misfiring. Replace if necessary (par 22). Leaks through the high tension wires may also be responsible, and they should be inspected (par 18). Make sure that the sockets in the distributor cap are thoroughly clean of corrosion and that the wires are fully seated.

[4] Check the operation of valve springs, and replace any that are weak (par 213).

d. Backfiring.
[1] As a general rule, backfiring into the muffler indicates too rich a fuel mixture and backfiring into the car-

buretor, too lean a mixture. Make necessary adjustments at the carburetor (par 55, 56).

[2] Check all fuel lines for restrictions (par 77), and clean the air cleaner (par 50). Clean carburetor if necessary, and check the float-valve level.

[3] Sticking valves or weak valve springs will also cause backfiring. Check for and correct these conditions (par 213). Make sure cylinder-head gasket is in good condition (par 214). Make compression test (par 9).

[4] Extremely late ignition timing will cause backfiring. Check timing, and make necessary adjustments (par 24).

8. MISCELLANEOUS ENGINE OPERATING FAULTS.

a. Excessive fuel consumption. This is usually caused by faulty carburetion. Inspect for fuel leaks first, then adjust the carburetor. Look for binding of the accelerator controls. Other causes may be the following:

[1] Excessive idling or driving unnecessarily in low gears.

[2] Overheating (par 89).

[3] Faulty mechanical operation. Check compression of the cylinders (par 9).
[4] Late ignition timing (par 24).

[5] Brakes dragging (par 274).

[6] Oversize or worn jets in carburetor.

b. Overheating. The most common cause is a defective cooling system. Refer to cooling-system trouble shooting (par 89). Other possible causes are the following:
[1] 0il with improper viscosity. (par 201).

[2] Too lean a fuel mixture (par 55, 56).

[3] Restricted carburetor air cleaner (par 50).

[4] Late ignition timing (par 24).

[5] Radiator restricted by bugs, weeds, or trash (par 95).

c. Excessive oil consumption.
[1] Make a thorough inspection for leaks. Check all oil lines, and tighten connections or replace as necessary {par 204}.

[2] Poor driving practices may be responsible and should be corrected. Speeding the engine will result in excessive oil consumption.

[3] Worn pistons or broken piston rings area common cause. Make the compression test (par 9).

[4] 0verheating may be a cause (par 89).

[5] Clogged crankcase ventilator may be a cause (par 207).

[6] Loose connecting rod or main bearings may be a cause.

d. Lack of power.
[1] The primary cause of insufficient power is poor compression. Perform engine compression test, and make the necessary corrections (par 9).

[2] The difficulty may lie in the fuel system, ignition system, or cooling system. Follow troubleshooting procedures for these systems.

[3] A clogged exhaust system or bent exhaust pipe may be responsible. Check for these conditions, and clean or replace pipes (par 84).

[4] Dragging brakes (par 274) or improperly inflated tires (par 247) may give the impression of too little power. Check for these conditions.

[5] Bearing failure in the power train may be responsible.

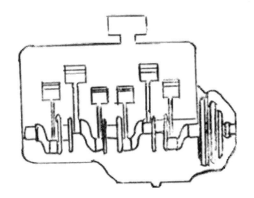

e. Operating knocks. Engine

noises generally termed as "operating knocks" can usually be narrowed down to one of the following:

[1] Overloaded engine. This noise occurs when an engine is placed under extreme load. Usually the noise will be reduced by shifting to a lower transmission gear. This knock may be due to a combination of causes, all of which can generally be remedied by using correct transmission speeds.

[2] Carbon knock. This knocking is caused by the accumulation of carbon in the combustion chambers which causes an increased compression ratio. It is most noticeable when the engine is hot and is accelerated (par 217).

[3] Timing knock. When the ignition is timed to operate too early it may cause a knock very similar to a carbon knock. The engine may also kick back when starting. Check the ignition timing, and make necessary corrections (par 24).

[4] Fuel knock. A poor grade of gasoline may cause a knock or ping similar to a carbon knock. Use a better grade of gasoline or readjust ignition timing (manual advance) to accomplish smooth running with the grade of fuel used (par 24).

[5] Pre-ignition knock. Among the causes of pre-ignition (auto-ignition) are the use of the wrong type of spark-plug and the presence of carbon deposits or sharp projections and corners in the combustion chamber. Make sure that correct plugs are used (par 17). Idle the engine for 30 seconds before turning off the ignition switch.

f. Mechanical knocks. Mechanical knocks are noises that result from wear or improper adjustments. These knocks are not always easy to locate accurately as no two engines have exactly the same sound with the same faulty condition. Experience and practice are required on the particular type of engine to be serviced. The first step is to be sure that the noise is in the engine. If the noise can be heard with the vehicle stopped and the clutch disengaged, the . fault is generally in the engine. The engine should be warmed up to operating temperature. Check to see that all cylinders are firing, then try the engine under load to bring out the knock. Eliminate first such possible causes as carbon and valves, and then check for the following:

[1] Crankshaft and bearing knocks. A heavy dull knock, most noticeable when the engine is accelerated under load, usually indicates loose bearings. This knock can generally be located by shorting out the cylinders on both sides of the loose bearing. End play is usually indicated by an intermittent knock which may disappear when slight pressure is put on the clutch pedal.

[2] Piston and connecting rod knocks. Knocks caused by a loose connecting-rod bearing can be shorted out. The slapping noise caused by a loose piston pin is most noticeable when the engine is cold; it too can generally be shorted out. The noise caused by a broken piston pin or ring usually has a sharp clicking sound and cannot be shorted out.

[3] Camshaft knocks. These knocks generally occur when the engine is going at half speed. The gear cover should be removed, and any play in the gears and shaft should be checked. Valve lifters and cam followers should also be checked.

[4] Timing - gear noises. A humming noise may indicate tight gears.

Loose gears and other timing gear faults are often indicated by a rattle or knock.

[5] Valve mechanism knocks. If valve-mechanism knocks cannot be eliminated by valve-clearance adjustment, remove the mechanism and check all parts.

[6] Water pump knocks. If knocks definitely point to the water pump, remove the assembly and repair or replace (par 98).

[7] Other engine noises. Check such possible sources of other noises as loose fan blades, the air compressor (par 287), the engine mounting (par 219) and rnuff1er parts (par 87).

9. COMPRESSION TEST.

a. Procedure. A test of engine compression will generally reveal the condition of pistons, cylinders, and valves. The compression test should be made with an accurate compression gage in the following manner:

[1] Operate the engine until norma1 operating temperature is reached (160° F or higher).

[2] Remove all spark plugs. Turn the ignition switch off and pull the hand throttle all the way out.

[3] Connect the compression gage

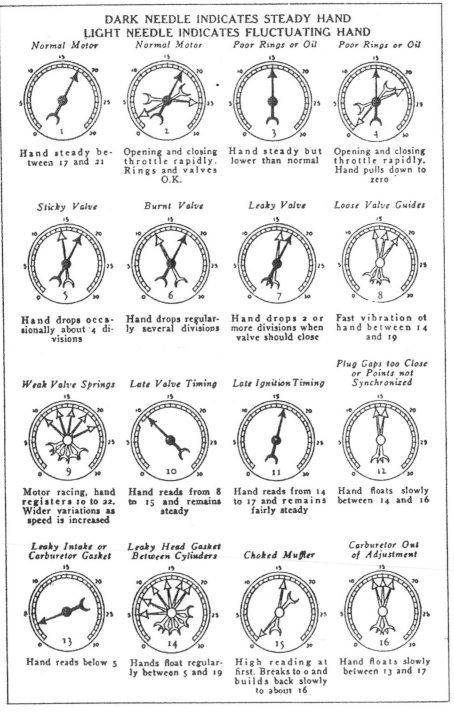

Figure 1. Interpretation of vacuum -gage readings

in one of the spark-plug holes. Crank the engine with the cranking motor and count the number of strokes required to reach a maximum reading on the gage (approximately 10 or 12 strokes). Record that compression reading for the cylinder.

[4] In the same way, take a compression reading for each of the other cylinders and record these readings.

[5] The compression readings should not vary more than 10 lb. The desirable compression will vary for different engines and is given in the engine specifications.

b. Diagnosis. If one cylinder has a low compression, the trouble may be in the rings or valves. Insert a liberal quantity of engine oil through the spark-plug hole of the cylinder with low compression. Allow a few minutes for the oil to spread around the piston, and then take a second compression reading. If the compression rises materially, the cause of low compression will be defective piston rings. An extremely low reading in two adjacent cylinders indicates a leak in the cylinder-head gasket or a cracked block.

10. VACUUM-GAGE TEST.
a. General. The vacuum gage can be a valuable aid in tuning an engine but cannot be used to isolate troubles unless the operator is used to working with one particular gage on one particular type of vehicle.

b. Connecting gage. To use the gage, disconnect the windshield wiper connection at the intake manifold and insert the vacuum-gage hose. On vehicles equipped with combination vacuum and fuel pumps be certain that the vacuum gage is connected to the manifold and not the windshield wiper connection. If the gage is connected to the vacuum pump a constant high reading will result in spite of any engine conditions prevailing. Whenever possible have the engine warmed up thoroughly before making a vacuum gage test.

Editors' Note: Of course, a vacuum gage will not do you any good if the vehicle doesn't have a vacuum source. For example, early jeeps do not have manifold that is tapped for vacuum access.

c. Interpreting results. The most common and reliable use of the vacuum gage is to indicate correct carburetor idling mixtures. It is also commonly used to assist in adjusting the valve lash of an engine. When using a vacuum gage, be sure to take into consideration all the conditions that affect it. For example: a low, steady reading might indicate poor compression or faulty carburetion; it might also be traced to late ignition timing. Many such examples exist, and only common sense can distinguish between the results of the tests. When several conclusions are reached, check those items which are most easily eliminated: ignition timing, carburetor idle adjustment, and valve lash. The chart shown in figure 1 will indicate some of the conditions most often found while using a vacuum gage.

Take it from Joe Dopes experience...just because your truck can doesn't mean it should. Preventive maintenance and proper care will keep your truck on the road for years to come.

No obstacle that he may meet
Ever forces Joe Dope to retreat,
For he thinks that a tire
Is immune to barbed wire —
Which it aint (any more than his seat)

Don't be a dope! HANDLE EQUIPMENT RIGHT

CHAPTER 3

ELECTRICAL SYSTEM

SECTION I BATTERY AND BATTERY CABLES

11. TROUBLE SHOOTING.
Battery failure is usually discovered when the cranking motor fails to operate. A simple, positive check of battery condition can be made with a hydrometer. If this test shows that the battery is fully charged, there may be a loose or broken cable. Defects that are not revealed by visual inspection can be localized by making line voltage tests.

12. BATTERY.
a. Specific gravity. Since the acid in the battery electrolyte decomposes as the battery discharges, the weight of the electrolyte gives a direct indication of the state of charge. This weight, or specific gravity, is measured with a hydrometer. To be accurate, the reading must be taken when the battery is filled to the normal level (3/8 in. above top of plates), but do not test the specific gravity for several hours after adding water . At extreme::? of temperature it is Important to correct hydrometer readings to allow for this variation. The normal standard is 80° F, but some batteries are corrected to 60° F. Add 0.004 for each 10° above the standard temperature, and subtract 0.004 for each 10° below standard.

b. Hydrometer readings. Test each cell with an accurate hydrometer. Each' cell of a fully charged battery should read between 1.260 and 1.300. Under normal operating conditions the battery should be removed and recharged if the reading is below 1.225.

c. Visual inspection. Inspect for cracks in the cell covers and containers or for cracked or chipped sealing compound. Slight cracks in

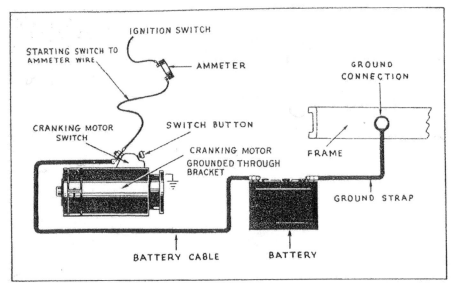

Figure 2. Battery circuit

sealing compound can be repaired by brushing lightly with a blow-torch ,flame. Cracks in cell covers, and container an d serious cracking of sealing compound require replacement of the battery.

d. Removal. First disconnect the ground strap to avoid a short if the wrench strikes the frame while removing the cable to the starting motor. If the bolts and nuts are corroded, hold the terminal with pliers and use a wrench on the nuts. This prevents damage to the battery posts. If the terminal clamp is not easily released, insert the screwdriver edge of a pair of pliers into

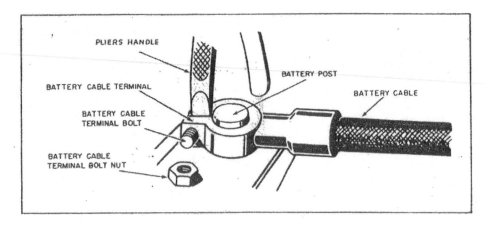

Figure 3. Releasing battery terminal yoke

the open end of the terminal yoke and twist to release the yoke (fig 3). Do not hammer the battery post to release the terminal. Do not place a screwdriver or other tool under the terminal and pry up on the terminal—this might break the cell cover.

e. Installation.

[1] Before installing the replacement battery, make sure the carrier is free from corrosion and has no tools or rocks in it. A tar-base paint can be applied to the carrier to assist in preventing corrosion. Determine the correct location of positive and negative posts before placing the battery in the carrier. The positive post is larger—may also be identified by a "+" or "POS" marking or by red paint on the top surface.

[2] If considerable corrosion has been encountered, washers cut out of felt may be slipped over the battery posts, the cables installed, and then the washers saturated with oil. After the terminals have been installed, a light coat of chassis grease may be applied around the correction to prevent corrosion.

[3] When installing the cable terminals, tighten the nuts carefully. Be sure the bolts are long enough to allow each terminal to fit the post correctly. Tighten the hold down bolts so that the battery cannot shift

in the carrier. Take care to avoid unnecessary tension that might crack the case of the battery.

[4] After the terminals have been tightened, check the installation by turning on the headlights with the engine not running. The ammeter should register discharge. 1ft he ammeter registers charge, remove the battery and install it in the reverse position so that terminals can be connected correctly.

13. BATTERY CABLES.
a. Examine the terminals and bat-

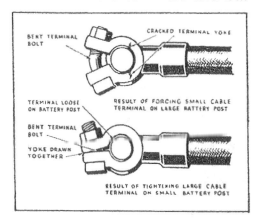

Figure 4. Result of incorrectly connecting battery terminal yokes

tery posts for signs of corrosion. Be certain that the nuts turn freely on the bolts and that .the bolts. are free. in the terminal yokes. Remove the bolts and examine them for corrosion and damaged threads. Use ammonia and water or soda (baking soda from a mess hall will do) and water to remove corrosion. Be careful to avoid spilling any cleaning solution into the cells; it will destroy the electrolyte. In the absence of these solutions, use a stiff-bristle or wire brush. Replace any terminals found cracked or excessively corroded; be sure to use terminals of the proper size (fig 4). If new terminals are soldered on the old cables, make certain that the old cable fits tightly into the new terminal and that the solder is applied with sufficient heat so that it is thoroughly worked through the strands inside the terminal.

b. Inspect the cables for worn insulation and broken strands of wire at the terminals and the points where the cables pass through openings in the frame. The insulation can be taped if replacements are not available.

c. Disconnect the battery ground strap where it is connected to the frame, engine, or transmission. Clean all surfaces of contact with a knife or file. Replace, making sure the bolt and nut fastens the ground strap or cable securely to the part that holds it. Use new lock washers.

14. LINE VOLTAGE TEST.
Excessive resistance caused by poor terminal connections or defective insulation will result in inadequate voltage at the cranking motor.

An abnormal drop in voltage can be detected with a low-reading voltmeter. Make these four tests (fig 5): (A) One prod of voltmeter on gr01.inded battery terminal and the other on vehicle frame, (B) one prod on ungrounded battery terminal and the other on cranking-motor switch stud, (C) one prod on cranking-motor housing and the other on vehicle frame, and (D) one prod on battery post and the other 0 n cable terminal. For each test, operate the cranking motor with the ignition switch off. If the voltmeter reading is more than 1/10 volt, there is excessive resistance. For (A), clean or replace the ground strap; for (B), clean or replace the cranking-motor cable; for (C), check the cranking - motor mountings and clean the contact surfaces on the switch; and for (D), remove terminal, scrape clean, replace, and tighten the bolts securely.

15. SPECIAL OPERATING CONDI. TIONS.
a. Tropical. When batteries are operated in tropical climates w her e. freezing temperatures are never encountered, the full-charge specific gravity is reduced to the value between 1.210 and 1.225 by dilution with water. Under these circumstances, a tag should be attached to the battery to show the full-charge specific gravity.

b. Cold operation. Battery capacity is greatly reduced by low temperatures. At 0° F the battery has only 40 percent of the cranking power it has at 80° F. Special care must be taken to keep batteries fully charged, but do not attempt to adjust specific gravity to values above 1.300. At temperatures below -20° F, batteries must be heated during periods of operation and stand-by.

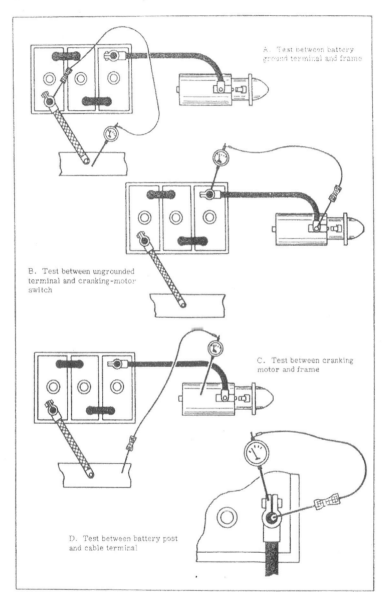

A. Test between battery ground terminal and frame

B. Test between ungrounded terminal and cranking-motor switch

C. Test between cranking motor and frame

D. Test between battery post and cable terminal

Figure 5. Line-voltage tests

16. TROUBLE SHOOTING.

Trouble in the ignition system is the most likely cause of engine failure. Because ignition operation is so closely related to engine operation, the trouble-shooting procedure is included in chapter 2. The following paragraphs give detailed procedures for the inspection of individual parts of the ignition system and for setting and checking the ignition timing.

17. SPARK PLUGS.

a. Removal. Spark plugs should be handled with extreme care to prevent damage to the porcelain. Before removing the spark plugs, clean the spark-plug recesses with a small brush or compressed air to keep dirt from entering the engine (fig 6). Use a socket wrench of the proper size and apply pressure on the wrench handle exactly parallel with the base of the spark plug (fig 7). Never use pliers or an adjustable wrench. Spark plugs with broken porcelain above the metal shell always indicate improper use of tools. If the spark plug resists turn-

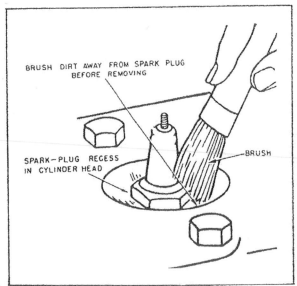

Figure 6. Cleaning spark-plug recess

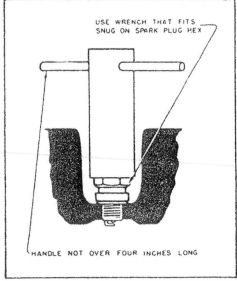

Figure 7. Removing and installing spark plug

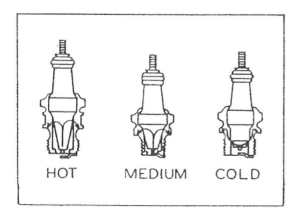

Figure 8. Path of heat conduction In spark plugs of different heat ranges

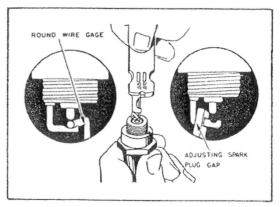

Figure 9. Proper method of adjusting spark plug gap

ing, do not force it. Turn it back and forth slowly until the threads are free. When extreme tightness is encountered apply kerosene or fuel oil to the threads and allow it to soak into them. This should free the threads.

b. Inspection. Spark plugs can be used for an accurate diagnosis of engine troubles. Cylinders which are pumping oil excessively will de. posit oil on the spark plug porcelain, where it is easily detected. Engines used for short "start and stop" driving periods will show a black, sooty carbon deposit on the inside porcelain and shell of the spark plug. Engines used constantly under heavy loads and engines operated when overheated will both produce a brownish film on the porcelain. The latter condition is also indicated by occasional "blistering" and cracking of the porcelain or excessively wide

spark-plug gaps. Examine the porcelain insulator for these cracks or blisters and the electrodes for fouling. Replace any spark plugs that are found to be in this damaged condition.

c. Heat transfer. Spark plugs must allow for correct heat transfer from the combustion chamber to the coolant in the cylinder block. Dirty or damaged spark-plug gaskets will hinder this transfer of heat and result in the spark plug's running too hot. This may be noticed by blistering or cracking of the porcelain or by the electrodes' being badly burned after a comparatively short period of operation. If spark plugs operate too hot after correct gaskets are installed, the engine may be running at higher than normal temperature. The radiator, fan belt, and water pump should be inspected. If these are not at fault, the spark plugs should be exchanged for ones of cooler operating characteristics as indicated by the number on the spark-plug porcelain (fig 8). Consult the vehicle specifications for the correct spark-plug number.

d. Cleaning. To clean spark plugs fouled with. carbon or covered with a brownish-grey powder, it is best to use a sand-blast cleaner of the type furnished by the manufacturer of the spark plugs. However, never use a sand-blast cleaner on aircraft-type, mica-insulator spark plugs. When such a cleaner is not available, scrape the carbon off the insulator and electrodes with a small penknife and then clean the spark plug in solvent or gasoline *(Editor: Even though it may have been a common practice during WW2, you should NEVER use gasoline as a solvent. You can obtain non-flammable solvents at your parts store.)* Use compressed air to blow away all traces of the cleaning solution and dirt.

e. Adjustment. When adjusting the gap between the electrodes, bend only the outside electrode (the one which is attached to the metal shell of the spark plug). Attempting to adjust by moving the center electrode will crack or break the insulator surrounding it. When adjusting the gap opening, use a round wire feeler gage of the proper size rather than

a flat one (fig 9). The older the spark plug, the more the material will have burned off the electrodes and the more spherical will be the space in which the spark jumps. For this reason a flat feeler gage will sometimes give an incorrect reading. Most spark-plug gap openings will vary from 0.020 in. to 0.040 in., depending on the vehicle. The average setting is about 0.025 in. Appendix I gives spark plug specifications and gap settings for various vehicles.

f. Installation. Be certain that each spark plug has a single gasket in excellent condition, preferably new. Screw the spark plug in the hole by hand. When the spark plug is seated, apply a socket wrench with a handle no longer than 4 in. Finish tightening by turning the socket by hand pressure for an additional one half to three-quarters of a turn. This will firmly seat the gasket without crushing it. Too much tension on the socket wrench will distort the sparkplug case and vary the gap. Make sure the terminals on the end of the spark plugs are firmly screwed on, and wipe any grease or moisture off the porcelain insulator.

18. HIGH-VOLTAGE CABLES.
a. Inspection. Examine these wires for any signs of frayed or damaged insulation, particularly where they

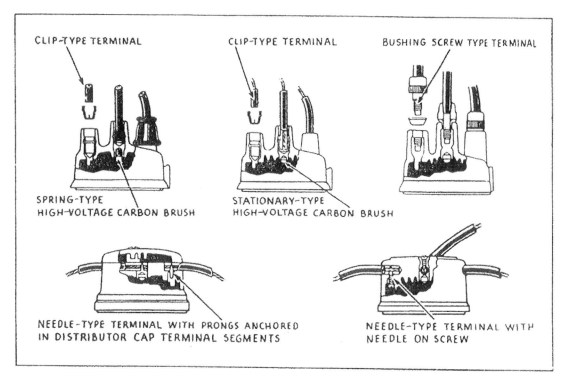

Figure 10. Types of high-voltage distributor terminals

enter a conduit or holder (fig 10). Examine the terminal ends of the wires for corroded or loose ends. Replace when such conditions are found.

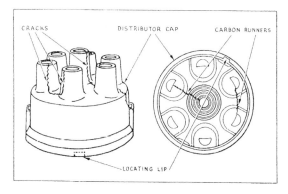

Figure 11. Cracked distributor cap

19. DISTRIBUTOR CAP AND RO-TOR.

a. Cap. Remove the distributor cap without removing the high voltage cables. Inspect the inside and outside for cracks and carbon runners (fig 11). These carbon runners are caused by the high-voltage spark's jumping and burning the material of which the cap is made. Moisture inside the distributor' cap is usually responsible. If cracks of carbon runners are found, replace the distributor cap. Emergency repairs may be effected by scraping out the carbon runner with a knife or sharp tool.

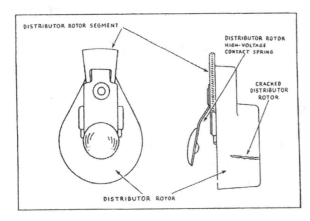

Figure 12. Cracked distributor rotor

b. Rotor. Remove the rotor by pulling it straight off the shaft. Inspect (fig 12) for cracks and carbon runners as in the cap. Make sure the spring that maintains contact with the distributor cap is in good condition. If any cracks or carbon runners are present, or if the spring is .corroded or weak, replace the rotor with a new one. The replacement must be the same size and type as the old rotor.

20. CONDENSER.

a. Inspection. See that the condenser is tight in the mounting bracket and that the pigtail is free of bare spots and frayed edges. Be certain the pigtail is firmly attached to the binding post and does not contact any moving part of the distributor.

b. Breaker points. If a faulty condenser is suspected, the breaker points will usually give an indication of the condenser condition. If the points are burned a deep blue or purple color and are covered with a scale, the condenser is shorted. If the points are excessively pitted, with a deep cavity on one surface and a corresponding built-up portion on the other surface (fig 13), the condenser is likely to be either under or over capacity. A vehicle will not run properly with a defective condenser, and replacement must be made. If a regular condenser is

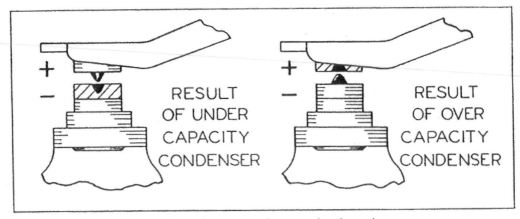

Figure 13. Effect of wrong condenser on breaker points

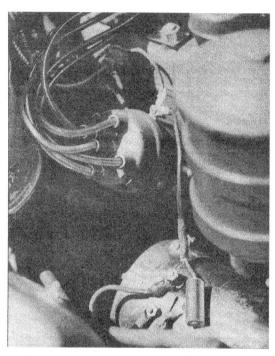

A burned out condenser in the ignition system may be replaced by the condenser on the generator or starting motor of a radio suppressed vehicle. Simply connect a short piece of insulated wire from the primary connection of the distributor to the condenser on the generator.

unavailable, any condenser may be used for an emergency. The radio noise-suppression condensers found on most vehicles will work satisfactorily until the proper condenser can be obtained.

c. Condenser tests. Several field-expedient tests may be made to determine the condition of a condenser.
[1] A test may be made for a shorted condenser with 110-volt alternating current and an ordinary light bulb. Connect the test light as shown in figure 14. If the light glows, the condenser is shorted and must be replaced. To check on the capacity of the condenser, strike the condenser pigtail lightly with the test prod; after a few seconds, bend the pigtail until the terminal touches the can of the condenser. A light spark should be noticed, accompanied by a snapping sound.

[2] Another method is to place the condenser on the engine of a vehicle which is idling and then bend the pigtail close to the terminal of one of the spark plugs. Allow, the pigtail to contact for only a second; then remove the condenser, being careful to avoid contact with the metal terminal of the condenser. After, a few seconds, bend the pigtail until the terminal touchos the can of the condenser; this should produce a slight spark, accompanied by the characteristic snapping sound. Occasionally the condenser may not be charged properly on the first try; a second attempt should always be made before condemning any condenser.

[3] To test the condenser without removing it from the distributor, crank the engine until the fiber rubbing block of the points in the distributor is midway between two lobes of the cam. Turn the vehicle ignition switch on and snap the con-

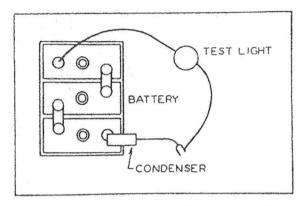

Figure 14. Use of test light to check for shorted condenser

tact points open and closed by hand; at the same time observe the contacts for evidence of flash. No arcing across the points will indicate a grounded condenser. A slight, barely noticeable flash will indicate

a normal condenser. A considerable arc or flash across the points will indicate an open-circuited condenser. In either case when the test shows the condenser to be defective, the unit should be replaced.

21. CONTACT BREAKER POINTS.

a. **Inspection.** Separate the breaker points and inspect the contact surfaces. Clean with a fine-cut point file if necessary, but be certain to remove all filings with a clean rag before using. When no file is available, use the sanded surface of a match box, a knife, or a sharp screwdriver blade. Make certain that the contact surfaces are strik-

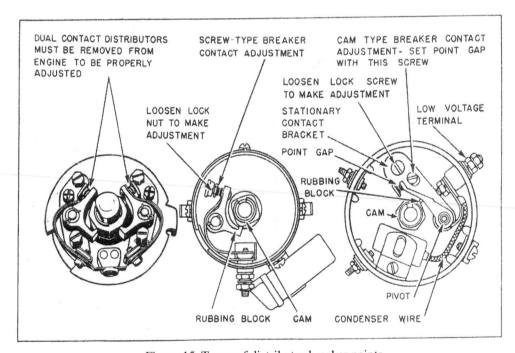

Figure 15. Types of distributor breaker points

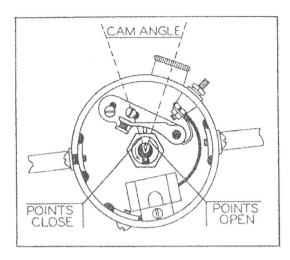

Figure 16. Carn angle is the angular rotation during which points are closed

ing squarely and evenly. If the faces of the contact points are not alined perfectly they cannot carry all the current necessary for good coil operation. To aline the contact surfaces properly, bend the stationary point arm or bracket. Never bend the movable arm; bending may weaken the arm and allow it to become bent and misalined in operation. Never grasp the point assembly so that any portion of the pliers or tool will touch the contact surface. Check the action of the movable arm on its pivot. It should move freely by hand against the spring pressure, and when released it should snap back into position. If sluggishness is noted in its operation during this test, the arm should be removed from the pivot and inspected for solidified grease or burrs obstructing its movement.

Clean thoroughly and apply a small amount of petrolatum" or light chassis grease before replacing the arm on the pivot.

b. Adjustment. To adjust the contact-point opening, crank the engine until the fiber rubbing block of the contact points is resting on the highest portion of anyone of the cam lobes. With a flat feeler gage inserted between the points, adjust the stationary point (fig 15) until a slight drag can be felt when working the gage back and forth between the surfaces. Select the proper thickness of gage after consulting the vehicle specifications. The gap will normally be between 0.015 and 0.020in., the average gap being about 0.018 in. One type of stationary point has the contact surface mounted on an arm which is securely fastened to the base plate of the distributor. The arm can be adjusted by loosening the locking screw and moving the adjusting screw (a cam head screw) until the desired opening is reached. Another type has the contact surface mounted on a machine screw which is threaded into a plate attached to the base plate of the distributor. To adjust this type, merely loosen the lock nut on the screw shank and turn the screw so the stationary contact moves nearer to or farther from the movable contact. Be sure to tighten the lock nut securely after, the correct gap opening is set, and always recheck, the opening to be certain that the point has not been moved in locking the assembly. After the assembly is locked, check the point opening for all the other lobes of the cam to make certain that the cam itself is not worn. Any variation of point-gap opening beyond 0.002 in. indicates a defective cam.

c. Cam-angle test. If the proper test equipment is available, the distributor should be removed and installed on a cam-angle testing machine. This machine accurately measures the degree of angular rotation (fig 16) in which the contact surfaces remain closed. Vehicle specifications include this angle, and in cases where the point-gap opening and the amount of earn angle differ, the earn angle should be accepted as being correct.

d. Replacement. When inspection indicates that contact-point replacement is necessary, use identical equipment. Always replace both contact points. In attaching the condenser leads and the movable breaker point spring to the binding post, take care that no part touches a movable portion of the distributor.

e. Spring tension. Weak or distorted springs on the movable breaker point result in a floating action that can cause engine misfire at high speeds. Points which have been so installed that they make the spring too tight will cause a bounding action at high speeds and give the same results. To check this condition, the spring tension can be measured by moving the movable point away from the stationary point wit h a small spring scale (fig 17). Accurate specifications for this tension are included in the vehicle service manual.

22. COIL.

a. Inspection. Ins p e c t the terminals to see that they are' clean and properly connected. If a defective coil is suspected, remove the coil and test it on the coil tester 17 -T-5576, or an equivalent instrument. All coil testers operate by comparing the coil with one of known characteristics. Instructions furnished by

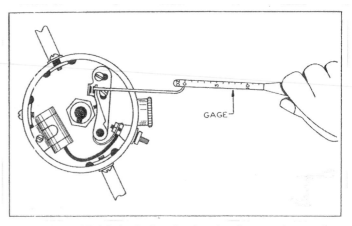

Figure 17. Method of testing breaker-lever spring tension

the manufacturer of the test instrument should be followed. No repairs can be made on the coil; if it is defective, it must be replaced.

b. Replacement. Disconnect the wires. Remove the nuts and washers that attach the coil bracket to the engine. Remove the coil, and replace it with one of the same size and capacity. If the coil has an enclosed terminal for the cable from the ignition switch, use a thin, flat tool. Slip the tool between the cover and coil; slide it around until the lock tongue is released, and turn the cover until it is released from the bayonet notches on the coil. To install an enclosed terminal coil, mount the new coil in the same position. Attach the terminal from the ignition switch. Slip the cover on, engaging the bayonet prongs with the slots in the coil cover. Push the cover all tho way on, and twist it until the lock tongue expands in the slot in the cover.

c. Emergency installation. If no tool is available to, remove an enclosed-terminal coil, an emergency installation can be made with an exposed-terminal coil. Place the new coil alongside the old one and tape the two firmly together. Transfer, the high-voltage cable and the distributor wire to the new coil. Connect a jumper wire from the other low-voltage terminal on the coil to either the ammeter outlet terminal or to the "live" terminal on the starter switch. Any available coil can be used in an emergency, but replace it as soon as possible with one of the correct type.

23. LOW VOLTAGE WIRES.
Inspect the wires leading from the distributor to the coil and from the coil to the dash panel in -the cab of the vehicle. Tape or replace any frayed, worn, or damaged wires. Inspect all electrical connections to insure that they are tight and clean. Dirty or loose connections cause high resistance to be added to the circuit and will seriously affect the amount of current which can flow in the wires. This is one of the most prominent causes of starting difficulties and faulty operation of engines. Connections can be checked quickly by attempting to move the wire which is attached to the binding post. If the wire can be rotated around the post easily, the connection is loose and should be tightened with a screwdriver or wrench. The metal terminals on the ends of the low-voltage wires should be firmly soldered for good connection (fig 18). A field expedient for a soldering iron can be improvised by removing the carbon electrode from a dry-cell battery and attaching a heavy wire to one end. Sharpen the other end to a point. Then attach a second wire to the part to be

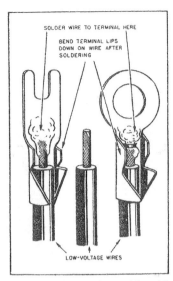

SOLDER WIRE TO TERMINAL HERE

BEND TERMINAL LIPS
DOWN ON WIRE AFTER
SOLDERING

LOW-VOLTAGE WIRES

Figure 18. Low-voltage wires with soldered terminals

soldered, and connect the two wires to a 6-volt battery. The battery in the vehicle may be used for this purpose. Touch the part to be soldered, and it will heat sufficiently to solder the connection. Always use a resin-core solder on electrical connections. Acid-core solder should only be used as a last resort. Never use acid-core solder on radio connections or interphone devices.

24. IGNITION TIMING.

a. Determining firing order. The firing order of an engine is usually indicated by numbers embossed on the cylinder head, exhaust manifold, or valve covers. If it is not given, it can be determined by the following method. First remove all the spark plugs. Then crank the engine by hand and observe when the no. 1

cylinder expels air. Note which cylinder is next to expel air; it will be the one that is next in the firing order. Proceed until all cylinders have been included. An easy way to do this is to fit paper plugs loosely in the sparkplug holes. When the engine is cranked by hand, the force of air on each compression stroke will force the paper plugs out of the spark-plug holes in the order of firing.

b. Locating top dead center. Crank the engine until the no. 1 cylinder is on top dead center of the compression stroke. This center can be determined by cranking the engine until a pressure is felt at the no. 1 spark plug hole. Continue cranking slowly until the pressure ceases. On the flywheel of some engines there is either a steel ball or an etched scribe mark which will appear in the inspection hole of the flywheel housing just before the piston reaches top dead center of the compression stroke '(fig 19). On other engines, this timing mark may be found on the crankshaft pulley on the front of the engine.

c. Installing spark plug cables. When top dead center of the no. 1 cylinder is located, remove the distributor cap. The rotor should be directly under, or near, one of the high voltage electrodes on the inside of the cap. Connect the cable from the no. 1 spark plug to the hole in the distributor cap which corresponds with this electrode. Connect the wires from the other spark plugs, in their firing order, to the distributor cap, proceeding around the cap in the direction of the rotation of the rotor. To determine this direction without cranking the engine, apply a twisting pressure to the rotor. The direction in which the rotor can be . turned against spring pressure is the direction of rotation. Connect the cable from the high-voltage outlet of the coil to the center hole in the distributor cap.

d. Initial timing. If the distributor has a manual advance, set it at 0. Be sure that the pointer is exactly in line with the mark on the flywheel or crankshaft pulley. Set the timing as follows:

[1] Engine not running. With the piston of the no. 1 cylinder on top dead center (timing marks alined), the points should be just opening. Loosen the distributor clamp and turn the housing in the direction of rotation of the distributor rotor until the points are closed. Turn on the ignition switch and hold the end of the high -tension cable that enters the distributor cap from the coil a distance of about 1/4 in. from a ground. Turn the distributor in the opposite direction to that of rotation of the distributor rotor until a spark jumps the gap from the high tension cable to the ground. At this time the points are just opening.

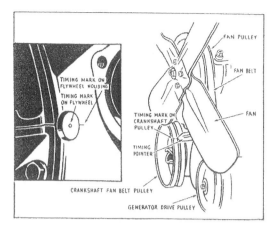

Figure 19. Flywheel and crankshaft timing marks

Clamp the distributor in this position. Turn the ignition off.

[2] Engine running. Replace the distributor cap. Attach one lead of a neon timing light to the no. 1 spark plug without disconnecting the high-tension cable. Connect the other lead from the timing light to a convenient ground. Start the engine and run at idling speed. Direct the beam of light on the timing mark on the flywheel or crankshaft pulley. Timing light flashes will make the timing marking appear stationary. 1t should be directly under the pointer. If it is not in this position, the timing should be adjusted until it is. To advance the timing, rotate the distributor housing in the opposite direction from the rotation of the rotor. To retard the timing, rotate the distributor housing in the same direction as the rotation of the rotor. When the timing mark and pointer are properly alined, clamp the distributor housing. If an ignition timing light is not available, a length of high-tension cable can be used. Place one end against the no. 1 sparkplug cable at the point where that cable comes out of the distributor. Hold the other end of the cable about 3/8 in. from the moving portion of the flywheel or crankshaft pulley. The spark jumping to ground will give much the same effect as a timing light.

e. Manual advance adjustment. A road test should be made to compensate for minor changes 0 f timing caused by variations in the gasoline from the fuel which the manufacturer intended to be used when the timing marks were put on the vehicle. With the engine warmed up, operate the vehicle at full throttle at a speed of 10 to 15 miles per hour in high gear. A slight amount of "ping" is not serious. If it becomes excessive, however, retard the spark by loosening the cap screw on the manual advance (fig 20) and moving the pointer toward "R". If there is no "ping" at all, advance the spark until it is just barely noticeable. Most vehicles are timed at the factory for 75-octane gasoline. For 70 or 72 octane fuel, it will be necessary to retard the spark about 3°. For 80 octane fuel, it will

be necessary to advance it about 3°.

f. Other timing faults. [1] If the distributor does not rotate when the engine is cranked, first check to see that it is firmly fastened all the way down in the mounting hole. If it is properly fastened and still does not rotate, inspect for a stripped distributor gear or oil-pump gear. It is also advisable .to inspect the camshaft gear.

[2] Occasionally the distributor is blamed for timing trouble which is caused by a worn or loose 'timing chain. This trouble can be detected by an explosion which occurs during the intake or exhaust stroke" and causes a popping noise in either the carburetor air horn or the exhaust pipe. To remedy this condition, remove the timing gear housing and replace or tighten the chain.

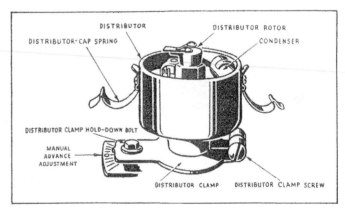

Figure 20. Distributor clamp and adjustments

25. TROUBLE SHOOTING.

The condition of the generator circuit (fig 21) is indicated by the charging rate and battery condition. The charging rate is 'shown by the ammeter on the instrument panel. If the ammeter does not give a clear reading, a test ammeter may be inserted in the circuit. The battery condition may be determined with a hydrometer. One of the following conditions will be found to exist:

a. Fully charged battery and low charging rate. This condition indicates that the generator and regulator are functioning properly. It can be verified by noting the charging rate shown on. .the .ammeter at a medium idle and then operating the cranking motor for about 10 sec-

onds (ignition off) to discharge the battery part way. Start the engine again and note the charging rate. Since the battery voltage is lowered, the generator output should show an increase for a short period.

b. Fully charged battery and high charging rate. T his condition indicates that the voltage regulator unit is not reducing the generator output as it should. Overcharging will damage the battery, and the excessive voltage in the electrical circuit may cause failure of the armature, ignition coil, distributor points, and lights. Remove the field lead from the field torminal on the regulator. If the output continues high, there is a short in the wiring or in the generator; if the output drops off, replace

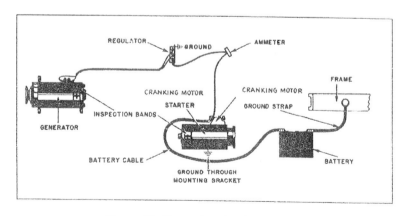

Figure 21. Generator circuit

the regulator. To isolate a short in the wiring or generator, remove the wire from the field terminal on the generator. If the output drops off, the short is in the wiring; if the output continues high, the generator must be replaced.

c. Low battery and low charging rate. Check the circuit for loose connections and frayed or damaged wires. These will cause high resistance in the charging circuit and make the voltage regulator act as if the battery were fully charged. If the trouble is in the wiring, temporarily bridge the armature and field terminals of the regulator with a jumper lead. Gradually increase the engine speed. Be careful not to let the generator output reach an excessive value; all regulation is removed under these conditions. If the generator output increases steadily with engine speed to or above its specified value; the regulator is defective. If the output does not increase, the generator is defective.

d. Low battery and no charging rate. Check first for loose connections and frayed or damaged wires. If they are not at fault, then bridge the armature and field terminals of the regulator as described above. Gradually increase the engine speed. If the generator begins to charge, the regulator is at fault. If there is still no charging rate, con-

nect a voltmeter of sufficient capacity between the armature terminal of the regulator and generator ground. If this voltmeter inidicates satisfactory voltage build up; the reverse current cut -out in the regulator is defective. If no voltage is shown, the generator is defective.

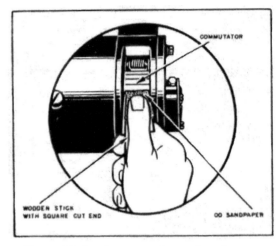

Figure 22. Sandpaper can be used to clean generator commutator

26. GENERATOR.

a. Inspection. If the tests listed above indicate a defective generator, inspect the following parts to determine if, one or more of them may be the:cause.

[1] Brushes. Remove ,the cover band and inspect the brushes. If they are badly worn or do not seat properly on the commutator, they should be replaced. An emergency repair may be effected by placing a small block of wood or several thicknesses of cardboard between the spring arm and the brush. This should be removed and new brushes installed as soon as possible. Emergency brushes can be improvised out of the carbon elec-

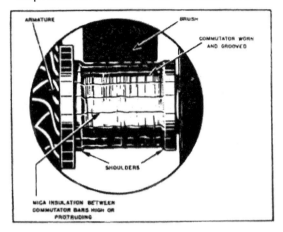

Figure 23. Worn generator commutator

trodes of certain dry cell batteries. If oil has solidified .around the holders and is causing them to stick, clean them with solvent or Diesel fuel applied with a small paint brush. Blow off with moisture free compressed air.

[2] Commutator. Inspect the commutator. If it is dirty, it can be cleaned with a strip of newspaper held against a small stick that is broad enough to cover the entire commuytator (fig 22). Never use emery cloth or crocus cloth. After cleaning, blowout all dust with compressed air. If the commutator is uneven or out-of -round (fig 23), it should be removed and turned down in a lathe. After this has been done, the mica or fiber insulation between segments should be removed to a depth of about 1/32 in. This operation can best be done with a hacksaw blade which has been ground to eliminate the kerf (offset of the teeth) in order not to exceed the thickness of the insulation.

[3] Drive pulley. The drive pulley may be of the cast or press steel type. Inspect the cast type for cracks or breaks in the casting. Premature failure of the fan belt may be caused by the scraping action of a damaged pulley. A pressed- steel drive pulley may also have cracks or be ,bent so much as to cause fan-belt wear.

[4] Fan belt. Inspect the bottom of the V-type belt to see that it is not shiny. A shiny surface indicates that the belt is riding on the bottom of the pulley grooves. A belt in this condition will slip. The belt should be properly adjusted (fig 24). If too loose it will slip; if too tight; it will cause excessive bearing wear. The most common adjustment is to allow 3/4 in. free play at a point midway between the water-pump pulley and the generator pulley.

b. Replacement. If the above inspection does not lead to the source of the generator trouble, there must be a ground, short; or open circuit in the armature or field and the generator should. be replaced and sent to a higher echelon for rebuilding. *(Editor: Of course today this means take to a shop that specialized in automotive electrics!)*

[1] Removal. Identify and mark each wire as it is disconnected from the generator. This is important since incorrect installation of the wires will, cause, seri:ms damage to the regulator and generator. With a belt-driven generator, remove the bolt from the adjustment-strap bracket. Then remove the bolts that secure the generator to the mounting bracket and lift the generator from the mounting. With a gear or coupling-driven generator, remove the set screw or holding strap and slide the generator from the mounting.

[2] Installation. Be sure the new generator is of the correct type, style, and voltage, style, and voltage, The battery terminal that is grounded is of, special importance and must be noted. With a belt driven generator, set the generator in position on the mounting bracket, and install the mounting bolts. Swing the generator toward the engine and place the drive belt on the pulley. Move the generator away

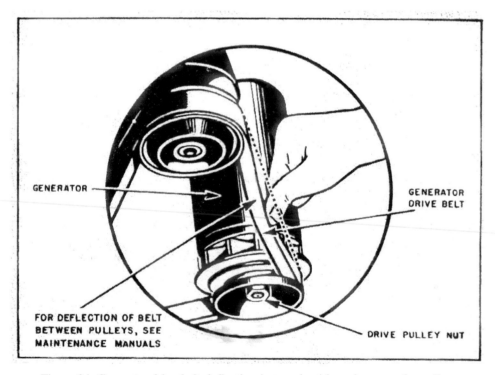

GENERATOR

GENERATOR DRIVE BELT

FOR DEFLECTION OF BELT BETWEEN PULLEYS, SEE MAINTENANCE MANUALS

DRIVE PULLEY NUT

Figure 24. Generator drive-belt deflection is tested midway between the pulleys

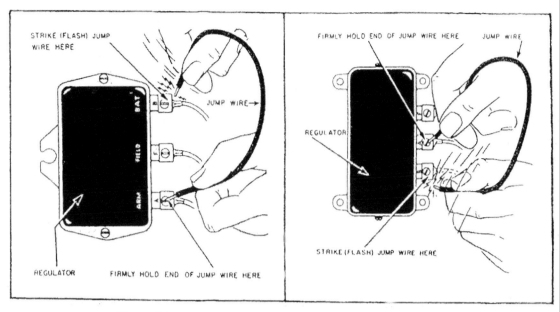

Figure 25. A jump wire is used to polarize a generator

from the engine until the proper belt tension is obtained, and, tighten the adjustment strap bolt. With a gear- or coupling driven generator, place the generator in a position that will not strain the wires when they are connected. Then start the drive gear in the timing gear-case opening and then install the generator into position. Be certain that the generator is tight against the timing gear case, and then install the set screw. With either type of generator connect the wires to their proper terminals and make sure the connections are tight. Then polarize the generator.

[3] Polarity. Whenever generator or regulator wires have been disconnected, the generator should be po-

larized after the units have been re-connected and before the engine is started. If this procedure is not followed, the generator or control box may be severely damaged. To polarize the generator, place one end of a jumper wire firmly against the armature terminal on the control box and then touch the other end momentarily to the battery terminal of the control box (fig. 25). This sends a surge of battery current through the generator and automatically gives the generator the correct polarity for the battery it is to charge.

27. REGULATOR.
a. Inspection. A defective regulator can be located by the trouble shooting procedure outlined at the

beginning of this section (par. 25). The regulator is a delicate instrument, and only a skilled mechanic should attempt to adjust. It or to locate any trouble within the regulator. Lower echelons should replace the defective regulator and return It to a high echelon for repair. *(Editor: Today this means that there is little you can hope to accomplishment by opening up your original voltage regulator. There are manuals that tell you what to do. About the best I can suggest that if you do not have experience in this area leave it alone—with the exception of taking a file (not emory but metal) and gently cleaning the electrodes—if you are certain they are sticking.)*

b. Replacement. To replace the regulator, first disconnect the battery cables or remove the battery connection from the regulator In the latter case, tape the end of the battery cable so it will not accidentally ground against the regulator or the frame of the vehicle. Then remove the other wires, marking each or noting their color so they can be properly connected to the new regulator. Remove the attaching bolts or screws, and lift the unit from Its mounting. Replace with a regulator that is exactly like the one removed If the replacement regulator does not have a flexible ground strap,

make sure the mounting surfaces are clean since the ground connection will be through them. When the regulator is in position, install the mounting bolts or screws and connect the wires, the battery wire last. Correct generator polarity as described m paragraph 26b.

28. AMMETER REPLACEMENT. Disconnect the battery cable before replacing the ammeter. Select an ammeter of proper size and style to make the replacement. The positive and negative terminals wlll probably be marked on the ammeter. If they are not, connect the wires to the new ammeter temporarily, connect the battery, and turn on the lights. If the ammeter registers a discharge, It is properly connected. Tighten the terminals with a wrench or screwdriver of the proper size. *The use of pliers for this operation should be avoided.*

29. TROUBLE SHOOTING.

Trouble in the starting circuit is always indicated by failure of the cranking motor. The usual cause is a defective battery (par. 12). If it is determined that the battery or battery cables are not at fault, then the trouble may be in the switch or the cranking motor itself. Inspect these units as outlined in the following paragraphs.

30. CRANKING MOTOR.

a. Inspection. [1] Brushes. Check brushes to see that they are long enough to touch the commutator completely in all positions. Inspect brush holders by lifting each brush and letting it snap back to position on the commutator. Any sluggish action should be corrected immediately. Clean the brush holder with solvent or Diesel fuel. After cleaning, be sure to blow the surface off with compressed air to eliminate the fire hazard. Tighten the pigtail terminal screws and inspect the pigtail insulation. Tape any exposed portion. Be certain that no part of the pigtails touch the metal parts of the motor. If brushes are worn too short to make adequate contact, replace the cranking motor.

[2] Commutator. Inspect the commutator for a worn brush path, burned spots, or excess grease. If the commutator is dirty, it can be cleaned with a piece of no. 00 sandpaper held on a flat stick and placed against the commutator while the cranking motor is operated for a few seconds. Never use emery paper or crocus cloth. If the commutator is not clean and bright after this operation, repeat the procedure. Blowout all loose particles with compressed air. If the commutator is burned or worn, it can be removed and turned down in a lathe. After this has been done, the mica or fiber segments should be removed to a depth of about 1/32 in. This operation can best be done with a hack-saw blade which has been ground to eliminate the kerf (offset of the teeth) in order not to exceed the thickness of the insulation.

b. Rotation. In order to inspect the cranking motor or to clean the commutator, it may be desirable to operate the motor when no assistant is available to press the starter button. This may be done from the en-

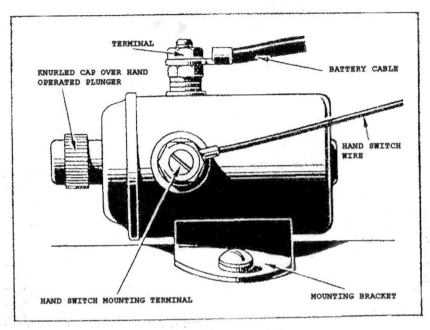

Figure 26. Solenoid starter switch

gine compartment in one of the following ways:

[1] Solenoid-type switch. Remove the knurled cap on the end of the switch (fig 26) and press the exposed plunger by hand. This posed plunger by hand. This will activate the switch and operate the cranking motor. On some solenoid switches the exposed terminal of the small wire leading to the starting switch may be grounded to the metal frame to activate the switch; on other solenoid switches the starter - button wire terminal and the battery-cable terminal may be bridged in order to operate the cranking motor.

[2] Overrunning - clutch - type switch. A switch of this type (fig 27) should only be operated after the gear on the cranking motor is in mesh with the flywheel gear. Use a large screwdriver or wrench as a lever to move the operating linkage in the same manner as though operated by the foot pedal in the cab.

[3] Exposed-terminal-type switch. This type of switch is usually placed on the floor of the vehicle cab (fig 28) and can be operated. from the engine compartment by bridging the exposed terminals with a heavy screwdriver or wrench. Since a current of several hundred amperes flow s through this bridge; it. must be made quickly and firmly, and broken quickly to avoid excessive

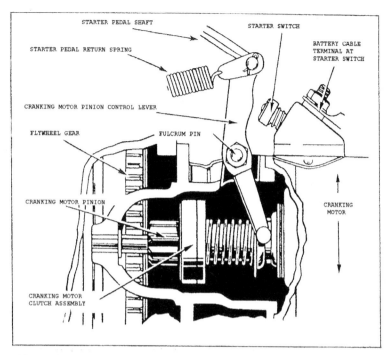

Figure 27. Overrunning-clutch starter drive with enclosed switch

arcing. *(Editor: instead of using a screw driver or using a wrench, obtain a remote starter switch at your auto parts store. While it may be unlikely there is a possibility of the sparks from the arcing igniting fuel or battery vapors—not a good thing.)*

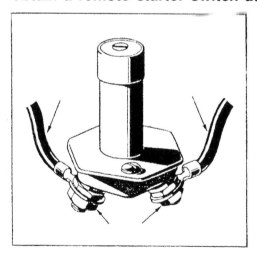

Figure 28. Exposed-terminal starter switch

c. Removal. First disconnect one of the battery cables to prevent shorting a cranking motor connection. If the starter button is on the instrument panel, remove the wire leading to it and mark this wire for easy identification. Disconnect the cable from the battery. Remove the bolts or nuts that hold the cranking motor to the engine. If there is a pedal linkage to the starter switch, remove that also. Move the free end of the cranking motor up and down to free the end in the flywheel housing and slide the cranking motor from its mounting.

d. Installation. Be sure that the replacement motor is the correct size, type, and model. If there is a switch on the housing, install that first.

To install the cranking motor, reverse the procedure of removal. Be sure that the mounting bolts and nuts are tightened evenly so that there will be no strain on the motor housing. As the last step, connect the battery cables. If it was necessary to remove accessories or oil lines in order to make room for the removal of the cranking motor, check the operation of these parts and inspect for any possible oil leaks.

31. CRANKING-MOTOR SWITCH.

a. Inspection. One cause for failure of the cranking motor to operate is a defective switch. On some type of cranking switches a quick check can be made by bridging across the switch terminals. On other types it may be necessary to disassemble the switch. Inspect the wiring and terminals to make sure all connections are tight. Inspect the contact surfaces of the switch for burning or corrosion. If there is a drive linkage from the starter pedal to the switch, see that this linkage moves freely and no cotter keys are missing.

b. Replacement. First disconnect the battery cables. Then disconnect the wires from the switch and remove the switch. On some models it will be necessary to remove the cranking motor in order to replace the switch. Use a wrench or screwdriver of the proper size to tighten the terminals. Avoid the use of pliers except in an emergency. Be sure to replace all wires that were disconnected in making the replacement. On linkage controlled starter switches, test the movement of the linkage before connecting the battery cables. The cranking-motor drive gear engages the flywheel gear completely before the contacts of the switch are closed.

SECTION V LIGHTING CIRCUIT

32. TROUBLE SHOOTING.

If the engine cranks and starts, there is current in the lighting circuit at least as far as the ammeter and any failure of the lights will be the result of failure in the bulbs or switches or in the wiring beyond the ammeter. The single wire from the ammeter to the light switch carries current to the entire lighting circuit. At the main light switch, the circuit is divided into multiple circuits, most of which include two or more lights. These go to junction points from which they branch out to single lights. In all cases the return path of the current is through ground. Thus lighting troubles may either be confined to a single light or two or more lights of a particular circuit or else they may apply to all the lights.

a. One light will not burn. This condition is the result of an open circuit or grounded wire between the light ground and the feed-wire junction. The specific cause may be a burned out or broken filament, a poor ground at the light, corrosion of the contacts or terminals, broken wire, or frayed insulation.

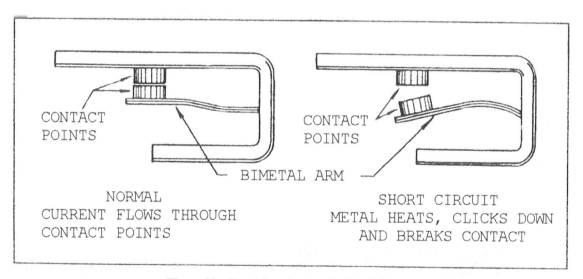

CONTACT POINTS

CONTACT POINTS

BIMETAL ARM

NORMAL
CURRENT FLOWS THROUGH
CONTACT POINTS

SHORT CIRCUIT
METAL HEATS, CLICKS DOWN
AND BREAKS CONTACT

Figure 29. Circuit breaker installed in lighting system.

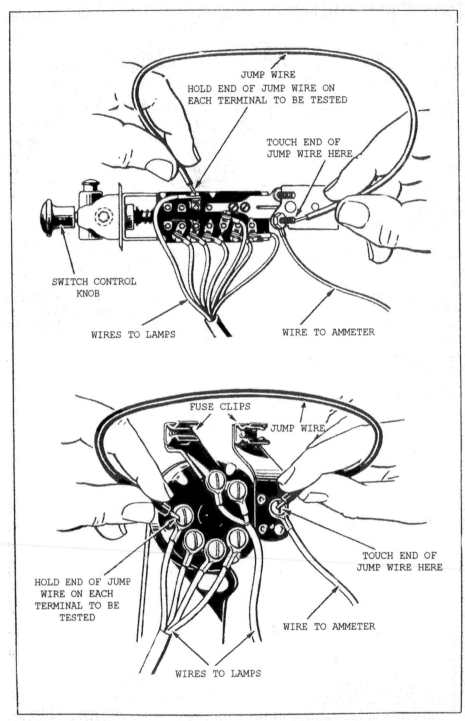

JUMP WIRE
HOLD END OF JUMP WIRE ON
EACH TERMINAL TO BE TESTED

TOUCH END OF
JUMP WIRE HERE

SWITCH CONTROL
KNOB

WIRES TO LAMPS

WIRE TO AMMETER

FUSE CLIPS

JUMP WIRE

TOUCH END OF
JUMP WIRE HERE

HOLD END OF JUMP
WIRE ON EACH
TERMINAL TO BE
TESTED

WIRE TO AMMETER

WIRES TO LAMPS

Figure 30. A jump wire is used to test main light switches

b. Two or more lights will not burn. The cause of this condition will, be located between the main light switch and the individual light junction. It may be a defective light switch, loose or corroded terminals, or broken wire.

c. All lights will not burn. If the battery is operating correctly, the cause of this trouble will lie in the part of the circuit common to all lights. It may be a defective switch, circuit breaker, or fuse; a loose or corroded terminal at the ammeter, or light switch; broken or frayed wire between the ammeter and light switch; or a ground at some point in the system which causes the fuse or circuit breaker to open the circuit.

d. Lights burn but give insufficient light. If not due to a weak battery, this condition may be caused by excessive resistance in the circuit. Look for loose or corroded terminals and contacts and for frayed insulation on the wires.

e. Frequent light failure. This is the result of excessive voltage at the lights and is caused by a defective voltage regulator.

33. FUSE OR CIRCUIT BREAKER.
This safety feature will be located on or near the main light switch. If a fuse is used, be sure that the end clips fit it tightly and that it is not burned out. A circuit breaker (fig 29) may be of the exposed-contact or enclosed-contact type. If the contacts are exposed, see that they are clean and fit properly. If the circuit breaker is defective, it must be replaced.

34. MAIN LIGHT SWITCH.
a. Inspection. Pull or turn the switch to the first position and observe the lights. Grasp the switch button and shake it slightly. If the lights flicker or go out, the internal contact is corroded or loose. Test the switch in this manner for each position. If any group of lights fails to burn, use a jumper wire (fig. 30) to connect the inlet side of the switch to the outlet terminal of that group of lights. The outlet terminal involved can be determined by referring to the wire color code in the vehicle maintenance manual or by noting the color of wire at the light which fails to burn. If the lights burn when the jumper is placed across the switch, the switch is defective.

b. Replacement. Disconnect the battery cable before starting to replace the switch. Remove the control knob and the mounting nut or screws. Lower the switch to a position where the terminals are in easy reach. Be sure the new switch is an exact duplicate of the old. Start at one end of the switch, and transfer the wires from the old switch to the

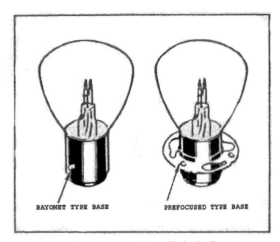

Figure 31. Two types of headlight bulbs

new, one wire at a time. When all the wires have been transferred, connect the battery and operate the switch. If it operates properly, mount it in position on the instrument panel.

35. WIRING.

All wires must be free from breaks, and the insulation must have no frayed or worn spots. The terminals should be clean, well soldered to the wire strands, and securely tightened to the switch and light sockets. Emergency repair can be made on damaged insulation by wrapping with tape, but the wire should be replaced as soon as possible.

36. HEADLIGHTS.

Two types of headlights are commonly used. In one type the bulb, reflector; and lens are contained in a single sealed unit. This is known as a sealed-beam headlight, and is the most common type. In the other type the bulb can be removed as a single unit. In this type a gasket is used to seal the lens and reflector together, when the headlight is assembled. The mounting may be either rigid or adjustable. The rigid type has two screws inside the headlight door to aim the beam. The adjustable type is moved as a unit to aim the beam.

a. Inspection. If a single headlight fails to operate, the bulb is probably burned out. If the bulb is not at fault, inspect the ground connection, the terminals, and the wiring to the nearest junction.

b. Bulb replacement. Remove the retaining screws and carefully take off the headlight door. Do not break the gasket or let the lens fall. If possible use bulb pliers to remove the bulb. If they are not available, either wear a glove or cover the bulb with a heavy cloth to protect the hand in case the bulb should break. Push the bulb in (fig 31) and twist it counterclockwise as far as it will go; then pull it straight out. If the bulb resists turning, push it in gently and twist it back and forth until it turns freely. Inspect the wiring before installing the new bulb. In order to do this, it may be necessary to move the reflector away from the headlight body. The bulb

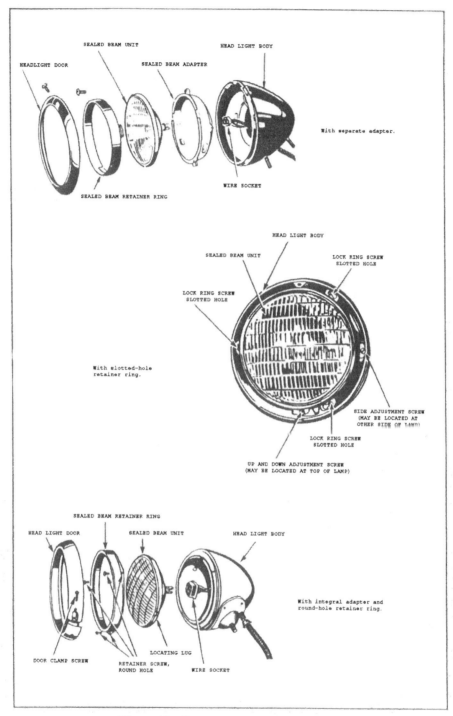

Figure 32. Construction of sealed-beam units

49

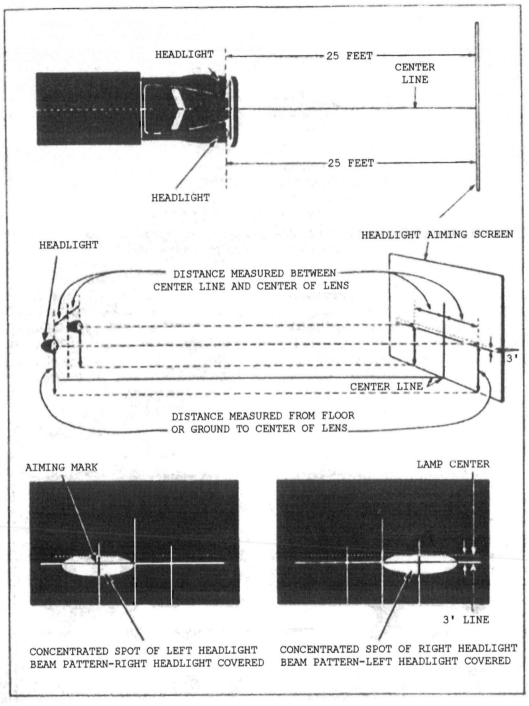

Figure 33. A screen or wall can be used to adjust the aim of headlights

flange of the new bulb is marked "top." Insert the new bulb, with this marking toward the top of the headlight. Push the bulb in, turn it clockwise, and then release it. If the contacts on the bulb catch and resist turning, withdraw the bulb, smooth the contacts, and reinstall. Be careful not to touch the polished surface of the reflector. Do not let dirt or grease get on the polished surface. Before replacing the gasket, lens, and door, switch the headlight on and see whether the bulb lights.

c. Sealed-beam replacement.

This type of headlight (fig 32) includes a door, retainer ring, sealed beam unit and headlight body. It may also include a sealed beam adapter between the sealed beam unit and the body. If the bulb burns out, the entire sealed beam unit must be replaced. Remove the door. The retaining ring is secured by three screws. If the holes in the retaining ring are round, remove the screws and the ring; if the holes are slotted, it is only necessary to loosen the screws and turn the ring until the large portion of the slot is under the screws. The sealed-

beam unit can then be pulled from the body, the connecter plug removed, and a new sealed-beam unit installed.

d. Adjustment. The headlight can be quickly and accurately aimed with a headlight tester. If a tester is not available, follow the procedure outlined below:

[1] Park the vehicle on level ground exactly 25 ft from and directly facing a screen or wall. This screen or wall should be marked with a vertical line or bar directly opposite the midpoint between the two headlights (fig 33). Measure the distance from the ground to the center of the head light lens, and make a

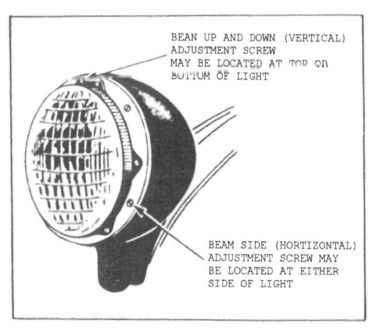

Figure 34. Adjustment screws on rigidly mounted headlights

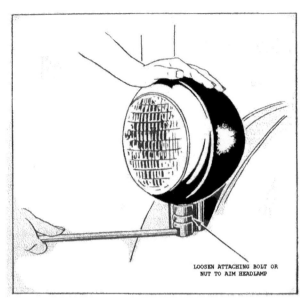

Figure 35. Adjustment of a headlight mounted on a bracket

ing screw will be on the right or left. If the headlight body is the adjustable type (fig 35), slightly loosen the attaching bolt or nut and move the headlight body until the beam is properly aimed. Tighten the attaching bolt or nut and inspect the beam to see that it has not been moved. Aim the other headlight in the same manner.

e. Dimmer switch. This is a foot-operated switch (fig 36) and controls the high and low headlight beams. On many vehicles an indicator bulb on the instrument panel burns when high beam is on. The switch can be inspected by turning the headlights on and pressing the dimmer switch repeatedly. The headlights should alternate between high and low beams. If they fail to

horizontal line or bar on the screen 3 in. below the level. Then measure the distance from center to center of the headlight lenses; and measure out half this distance on the horizontal line from the vertical center line on the screen.

[2] Turn on the headlights. If necessary depress the dimmer switch until the lights are in the high beam position. Cover the light not being adjusted with cloth or paper. If the light body is the rigid type (fig 34), remove the door and turn the adjusting screws until the center of the beams at the point where the appropriate horizontal and vertical lines cross. The vertical adjusting screw will be at the top of bottom of the light body; the horizontal adjust-

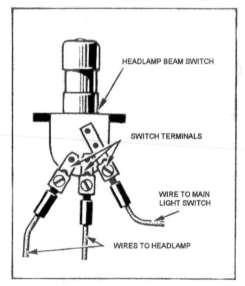

Figure 36. Headlight beam switch mounted on floorboard

burn in one or both positions or fail to change properly, use a jumper lead to short out the switch by connecting the inlet terminal from the main light switch with first one and then the other of the two outlet terminals. If lights work properly replace the switch.

37. BLACKOUT DRIVING LIGHT.

This is a sealed-beam type of light and is mounted on the left fender to the left of the headlight. It may either be controlled directly by the main light switch or by a push-pull type of switch on the instrument panel (marked "B.O. Drive") that will operate when the main light switch is in the blackout position.

38. BLACKOUT LIGHTS. These
lights (fig 37) are mounted on the fenders at the side of each headlight. They are controlled by the main light switch and burn when the main light switch is in the blackout position. Bulbs can be replaced in the same general manner as for headlights.

39. STOP AND TAILLIGHTS.
These lights are mounted at the rear corners of the vehicle. The left hand light includes a combination stop and-taillight unit and a blackout taillight unit. The right hand light is the same except that the stoplight is

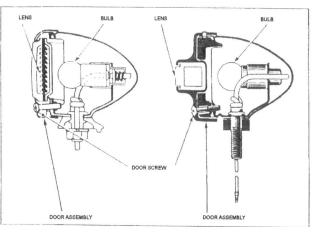

Figure 37. Two types of front blackout lights.

omitted. Construction of these lights may be either sealed-beam type or plain.

40. STOPLIGHT SWITCH. The
stoplight switch may be operated either hydraulically or by compressed air, depending upon the type of brakes used. Current is supplied through the main light switch, which must be turned on for the stoplight to operate. To test, press the brake pedal and see if the stoplight burns. If it does not, connect a jumper lead across the switch terminals. Then if the stoplight burns, the switch is defective and must be replaced; if it does not burn, the trouble is elsewhere.

a. Hydraulic switch. This type of switch (fig 38) is located on the master cylinder of the brake system. It will not work unless the brake sys tern is filled with fluid and operating properly. Inspect for fluid

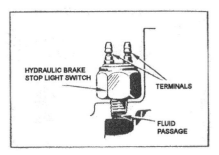

Figure 38. Hydraulic brake stoplight switch

1eaks around the switch by applying the brakes and watching for bubbles at the point where the switch is attached to the brake cyl-

inder and at the end plate of the switch. Before removing the switch, be sure the brake pedal is off. Do not depress the brake pedal while the switch is removed. In order to keep the brake fluid from draining from the cylinder, have the new switch ready and install It as soon as the old one is removed. Use a wrench that fits the switch body tightly.

b. Compressed air switch. When compressed air enters this switch (fig 39) as the brake pedal Is depressed, it forces the switch diaphragm to move and close the circuit. If the stoplight fails to light, use a jumper lead to short out the switch; if the light now burns, the switch is defective. The contact points can be inspected by releas-

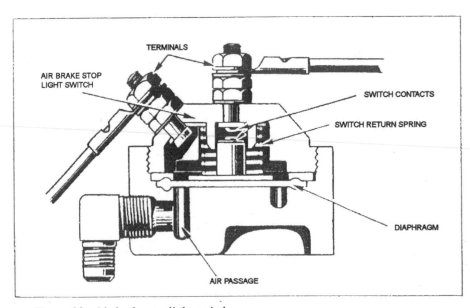

Figure 39. Air-brake stoplight switch

ing the air from the reservoir, disconnecting the wires from the terminals, and removing the threaded upper section of the switch with a wrench. Clean the contact points with a fine file or with sandpaper, and reassemble the switch. It is not necessary to fill the air reservoir to full capacity to test the switch; about 5 pounds of pressure is sufficient. If the switch still fails to function, it will have to be replaced. Release the air from the reservoir, and disconnect the wires from the switch terminals. Disconnect the tubing from the bottom of the switch. Use two wrenches one to keep the connection from turning, the other to remove the nut (fig 40). Replace the switch and reconnect the air connection. Start the nut by hand, and then finish tightening with a Wrench.

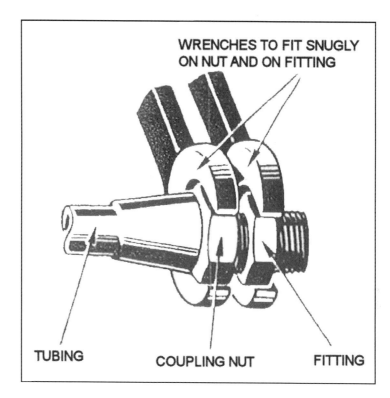

Figure 40. Use two wrenches to loosen this type of connection

41. INSTRUMENT PANEL LIGHTS.

The Instrument-panel lights are controlled through the main light switch and may have an additional push-pull or toggle switch so they can be turned off when the headlights are on. These lights and this switch are tested and replaced in the same general way as other lights and switches. The exact location and method of changing instrument-panel lights varies with different vehicles. In most cases the socket is removed from the light case and then the bulb removed from the socket.

55

42. TROUBLE SHOOTING.

If current from the battery' is reaching the horn relay but the horn fails to sound when the button is pressed, test the horn circuit as follows: Use a short length of jumper wire and gr6un.d the switch (S) terminal of the .horn relay (fig 41). If the horn sounds, the horn button is defective. If the horn does not sound, use the jumper to connect the battery (B) and horn (H) terminals of the horn relay. If the horn now sounds, the horn relay is defective; if the horn does not sound, the horn is defective. When the horn button or the horn is defective the trouble may be in the wires leading to these units. Inspect this wiring and the terminals.

43. HORN.

a. Inspection. See that the mounting bolts are tight. A rubber mounting should be replaced if it is broken or squeezed out of shape. Check the terminals and wiring.

b. Adjustment. Remove the back shell from the horn to be adjusted.

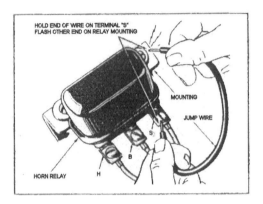

Figure 41. A jump wire is used to test the horn circuit

Loosen the lock nut on the adjusting screw, and turn the adjustment about one-eighth of a turn. Tighten the lock nut and test the horn. Adjust until the note is loudest. On dual horns, disconnect the horn that is not being adjusted.

c. Replacement. Disconnect the battery cable before replacing the horn. Disconnect the horn wires from !:he horn, and then remove the horn from the bracket.

44. HORN RELAY.

a. Inspection. Tighten the horn-relay mounting bolts and the relay terminals. Be certain that the cover is firmly fastened to the relay. If there is a fuse, inspect it and see that the holder clips make good contact. If the relay is not operating properly, the cause may be corroded contacts. Remove the cover, and sand or file the contacts before removing the cover, always disconnect the battery or remove the battery wire from the relay.

b. Replacement. Before removing the horn relay either disconnect the battery or disconnect the battery wire and tape the end to keep it from grounding accidentally.

45. ,HORN BUTI'ON.
a. Types. Two general types of mountings are used for horn buttons. In one type, two or three screws enter from the under side of

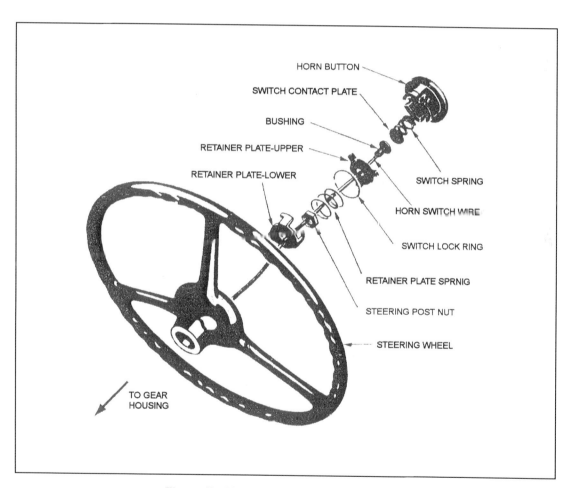

Figure 42. Pin or lug retainer horn-switch button

the steering wheel and engage a retaining ring which holds the button in place. In the other type the horn button is held by a lock ring and three lugs (fig 42).

b. Removal. The horn button is removed by one of the following methods:

[1] Screw. type retainer. Disconnect the horn-switch wire at the bottom of the steering-gear housing. Remove the retaining screws. Hold the retainer ring with one hand to avoid damage to the threads. Note the relative position of the horn-button spring retainer ring, and button so that they can be replaced in the proper order.

[2] Lock-ring retainer. Disconnect the wire at the bottom of the steering-gear housing. Press the horn button as far down as it will go, and turn it to the left or right until the pins or lugs can be felt to strike the sides of the slots. Release the pressure, and the button will be forced out of the steering wheel by the spring.

46. HORN. SWITCH WIRE.
a. Types. If the wire is connected to a terminal on the steering column tube at a point 6 in. above the steering-gear housing, it is soldered to a contact sleeve on, but insulated from, the main steering-gear shaft.

In this case the steering assembly must be removed from the vehicle in order to remove the horn-switch wire. Other types of horn-switch wires may be removed without disassembling the steering gear.

b. Removal. Disconnect the horn wire at the bottom of the steering. gear housing. Tie a string to the end of the wire. Remove the horn button. The insulator bushing can then be removed and the wire pulled out of the steering column. As the wire pulled out, the string will be pulled up through the column. Untie the string from the wire and attach it to the new wire. The new wire can now be pulled down through the steering column by the string.

An army truck being repaired at a mobile unit in England. Note the caution sign on this American vehicle from a "keep to the right" country, now in a "keep to the left" one. Photo credit: Library of Congress, 1942.

You never know when the need for trouble shooting will occur. Most likely, it will happen when you can least afford the delay. Preventive maintenance is your best ally to see that these surprises don't happen. But if they do hopefully the hints and tips in this manual will help you "keep them rolling."

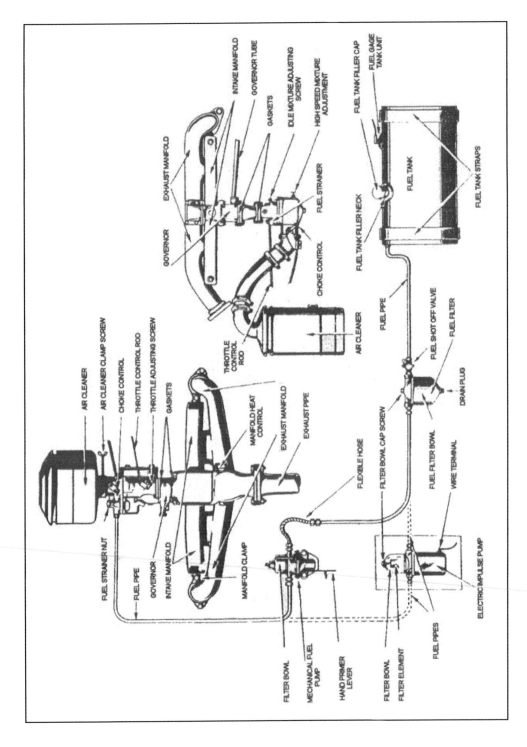

Figure 43. Fuel system

CHAPTER 4

FUEL SYSTEM

SECTION I AIR CLEANERS

47. TROUBLE SHOOTING.
Obstructions in the air passages retard the flow of air to the carburetor and may bring about too rich a fuel mixture. This condition may cause a sluggish engine, smoking exhaust, and loss of power. Examine the cleaner body and the air-intake ports for signs of dust, dirt, and oil. I! these elements are pre-

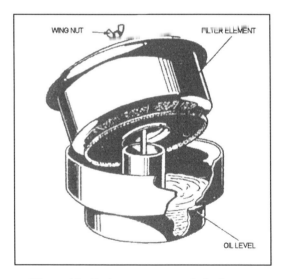

Figure 44. Carburetor-mounted air cleaner

sent, they indicate the air cleaner is dirty. It should be disassembled and cleaned thoroughly.

48. INSPECTION.
Inspect the level and condition of oil in the reservoir. To inspect the oil level in the carburetor-mounted type of air cleaner (fig 44), it is only necessary to remove the wing nut at the top of the cleaner housing and then lift off the cover and filter element. In the through-bolt type (fig 45), the wing nut is an integral part of a bolt which is threaded into the lower part of the housing or bracket; this type must be removed as a complete unit and then disassembled to inspect the oil. The dash-mounted type of cleaner (fig 46) has a detachable reservoir at the bottom. Inspect the bracket anchorage for breaks or cracks. Shake the cleaner by hand, and apply a wrench to the bolt heads to see that

they are tight. Tighten the clamp screw if the cleaner is attached to the carburetor air horn. Tighten the wing nut at the tap or any Wing nuts holding on the oil reservoir.

49. REMOVAL.
a. Carburetor mounted type. Loosen the wing nut clamp, or screw clamp at the base of the cleaner and remove the cleaner as a unit. This cleaner may have an additional brace fastened to the engine block or head for additional security. It is necessary to release the clamp and remove the. brace bolt to remove the cleaner.

b. Through-bolt type. Unscrew the bolt and remove the cleaner as a unit. An updraft-type cleaner is usually mounted on a bracket and connected to the carburetor with a tube. Release the hose clamps and the bracket bolts to remove the cleaner.

c. Dash-mounted type. This type of oil cleaner is usually larger than the others and is the self-washing

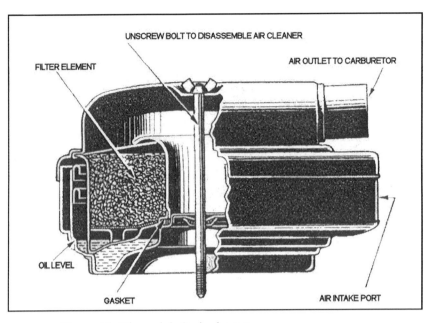

Figure 45. Through bolt air cleaner

type; the filter element does not require cleaning. It is only necessary to remove the oil reservoir to service the cleaner.

50. CLEANING.
a. Drain the oil and scrape the dirt from the reservoir. Wash the filter element if necessary, allow it to drain for a few minutes, and re-oil with engine oil.

b. Wash the cleaner reservoir and wipe it dry.

c. Fill to the proper level. The oil level is shown in various ways. There may be a mark on the side of the reservoir or an offset in the metal housing. On some types of air cleaners, the upper half of the reservoir is rolled outward in a beveled section, and the top of the inside margin of this section represents the oil level. On other cleaners the oil reservoir consists of an inner and outer cup marked with lines which indicate the proper level.

51. REPLACEMENT.
a. Handle the cleaner carefully, holding it level to prevent the oil from spilling. Place it in position and tighten the clamp screws and brace.

b. If it is attached with a tube (such as the updraft type), connect the tube carefully, and be certain that the connection forms an air tight seal.

c. If it is the dash-mounted type, be certain that the main body of the cleaner has been wiped clean before placing the reservoir in position and be sure the catches holding, the reservoir are secure.

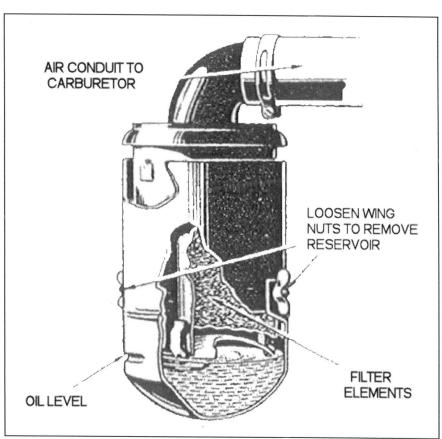

Figure 46. Dash-mounted air cleaner

52. TROUBLE SHOOTING.

Failure of the engine to operate is rarely caused by carburetor defects. If it is determined that the carburetor is responsible (that is, the ignition system is working properly and fuel is reaching the carburetor), the carburetor may be clogged or the float level may be improper. The only adjustments the second and third echelons can make on the carburetor are adjustments of the idling speed, the idling mixture, the choke control mechanism, and the accelerator pump seasonal adjustment.
(Editor: This is true for the home mechanic as well. Although you could experiment with changing valve sizes but that is beyond the scope of this book.)

Improper adjustment should not prevent engine operation but proper adjustment is necessary for maximum operating efficiency.

53. INSPECTION.

a. **Connections.** Look for leaks at the fuel-line connections. If any leakage cannot be stopped by drawing (tightening) up the union nut, there may be a split tube or a poor seat in the union. A damaged flare should be cut off and a new flare made with a flaring tool. Packing with string may serve as a temporary repair. If the fuel contains a dye, a fuel leak may be indicated by an. accumulation of the dye. But it should be remembered that the porous metal used for some castings sometimes permits a small amount of seepage, and an accumulation of dye may be due to this rather than a fuel leak. Leakage may be caused by a split adapter, in which case temporary repair can be made by soldering. *(Editor: Use extreme caution when using HEAT or SPARKS around the carburetor or anything with fuel or fuel vapors. Use YOUR good judgment and common sense.)*

b. **Fuel bowl.** Fuel seeping out around the fuel-bowl cover indicates a loose cover, a damaged gasket or casting, or a defective float valve. Slight seepage is probably due to a loose cover. Extensive seepage is likely to be caused by a defective float valve.

[1] Remove the fuel-bowl cover to examine the floats. If the float con-

tains fuel, causing it to lose buoyancy, determine where the fuel entered the float and drill a small hole (1/8 in.) at this point. Drain the fuel from the float, and patch the hole with a light drop of solder.

(Editor: Use extreme caution when using HEAT or SPARKS around the carburetor or anything with fuel or fuel vapors. Use YOUR good judgment and common sense.)

[2] If the float needle valve and seat show indications of wear, replace them with new parts and new gaskets. From the specifications of the carburetor determine the correct float level, and set the float by bending the float support arm. Hold the float in the closed position and blew into the fuel-line adapter. No air should pass through the valve.

[3] Examine the gasket. Replace it if there are any breaks or hardened sections. Be sure the new gasket does not obstruct any apertures in the housings. Draw, down the cover screws evenly.

c. Plug caps. Inspect all caps covering the check valves and jets. Tighten any of these that leak. Tighten the flange nuts or cap screws holding the carburetor to the manifold assembly.

d. Carburetor fuel strainer. Remove the fuel strainer from the carburetor or the cover from the strainer. Wash the strainer with cleaning fluid and a brush and dry it with compressed air. Examine the strainer gasket, and replace if compressed or damaged.

54. THROTTLE CONTROL.

a. Updraft inspection. The range of throttle opening can be determined by operating the hand throttle or accelerator pedal. The opening range should extend from the point where the idle screw contacts the stop to where the throttle-lever stop contacts the full-open-position lug on the carburetor body. Operate the throttle control to be certain the throttle will range from idle to full open position. Examine the carburetor control levers and the rod leading from the acceleralor to the controls. These controls must be free at all connections and should not bind or rub against the engine or the floorboards. The accelerator is returned to closed position by a coil spring. Be certain this spring is not damaged, or disconnected, it must be firmly attached to the throttle lever and to the spring pivot pin.

b. Downdraft inspection. When a downdraft carburetor is used, the range of throttle opening is determined by the following steps: Remove the air cleaner. Set the choke valve to full open position. Should the choke be automatic, the valve must be held open unless the engine has been thoroughly warmed. Open and close the throttle. Observe the action of the throttle valve at the carburetor. The valve should be in a parallel position (fig 47) to the flow of fuel when the accelerator pedal is :fully depressed or when the hand-throttle control is open to the limit.

c. Adjustment. For either updraft or downdraft carburetors. adjust the length of the accelerator control rods at the throttle-valve lever to obtain the full operating range. The hand-throttle adjustment is made as follows: Tighten the throttle control assembly at the instrument panel. Loosen the screw on the throttle control-wire stop collar or swivel clamp. Tighten the clamp holding the conduit. Place the throttle valve in the idle position, and push the throttle valve on the instrument panel all the way in. Tighten the swivel clamp or position the collar about 1/4 in. below the throttle lever and tighten the! lock screw. Test for open and closed positions of the throttle.

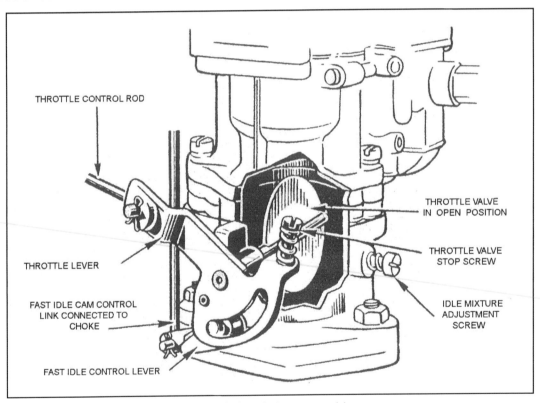

THROTTLE CONTROL ROD

THROTTLE VALVE IN OPEN POSITION

THROTTLE VALVE STOP SCREW

THROTTLE LEVER

FAST IDLE CAM CONTROL LINK CONNECTED TO CHOKE

IDLE MIXTURE ADJUSTMENT SCREW

FAST IDLE CONTROL LEVER

Figure 47. Carburetor with throttle in open position

d. Accelerator pump stroke adjustment. On some carburetors an adjustment is provided for the length of stroke of the accelerator pump. The connector link on the accelerator pump arm can be located in one of three positions. The long stroke is used for cold climates, high altitudes, or high-test fuel. The medium stroke is used for normal temperatures and operating conditions. The short stroke is used for hot-weather operation. To make the adjustment, it is necessary to remove the a1r-mlet section of the carburetor.

55. MANUAL CHOKE CONTROL.
a. Inspection. Examine the action of the choke valve to be certain it operates at full range from open to closed position. When the choke valve or disk has a spring-loaded poppet valve as a part of the disk, be certain the valve is free on the supporting stem and that the spring holding the valve in place is not damaged.

b. Straightening conduit. Should the choke control fail to operate/ the choke-Wire conduit may be sharply bent, causing the wire to bind. When this occurs, loosen the clips

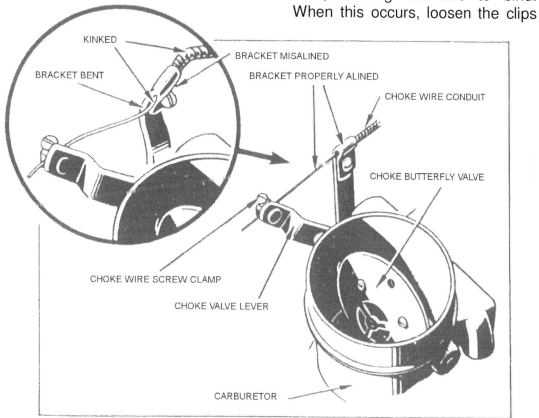

Figure 48. Alinement of carburetor choke control

holding the conduit and move it to a position in the clip that avoids any sharp bend. If the bind is caused by a sharp kink in the conduit and not by improper placing of the holding clips (fig 48), grasp the conduit with both hands, with a thumb and finger on each side of the kink, and bend it straight. Drop some penetrating oil or a mixture of kerosene and engine oil at several places along the choke wire conduit. *(Editor: It is not advisable to use kerosene or other combustible.)* The oil will gradually seep through the spiraled coils of the conduit and lubricate the wire.

c. Adjustment. Tighten the nut holding the choke control to the instrument panel. Push the choke button in. Tighten the stationary conduit clamp at the carburetor. Loosen the set screw in the choke wire swivel clamp. Hold the choke valve fully open and tighten the swivel clamp against the wire (fig 49). Test for extremes of travel as the choke button is moved out from the full open to the full closed position.

d. Replacement.
[1] Should it be necessary to replace the control assembly, loosen

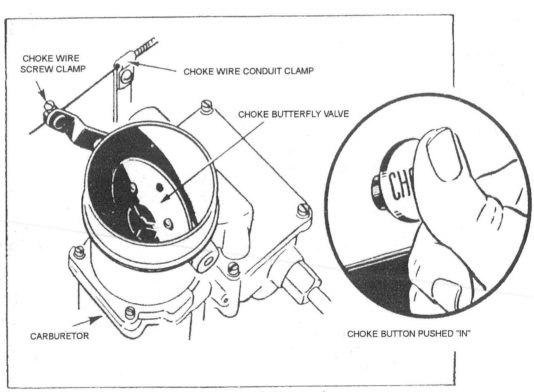

Figure 49. Carburetor choke control

the choke wire swivel clamp screw, the choke-wire conduit-clamp screw (fig 49), and; any other clamps that support the conduit. Unscrew the nut holding the choke control in the instrument panel. This nut is located behind the panel. Pull the unit and the conduit from the instrument panel. The replacement part should be identical to the unit removed. However, if a universal unit is used, it may have to be shortened to conform to the old part.

[2] To shorten a conduit, withdraw the control wire and file or grind a mark at the point where it is to be broken. Hold the conduit with pliers on each side of the mark. To make the break, bend the conduit sharply several times.

[3] To install the assembly, replace the control wire m the conduit, remove the jam nut on the control button, run the conduit through the instrument panel, and replace the nut on the assembly. When running the conduit through the fire-wall, be careful to prevent any sharp bends which may cause the wire to bed.

[4] To connect the control to the carburetor, place the conduit in the

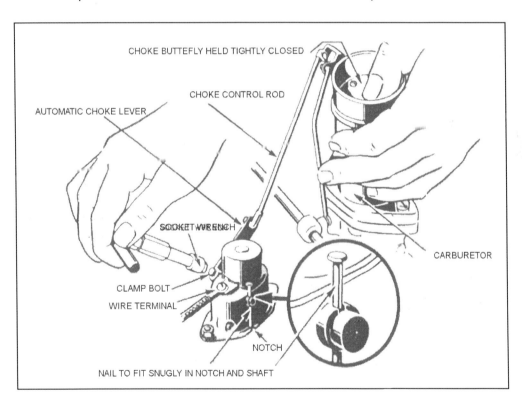

Figure 50. Adjustment of electric choke

carburetor bracket and tighten the clamp screw. With the choke in the full open position and the control button in, enter the wire in the swivel clamp on the choke-valve lever and tighten the screw in the clamp.

56. AUTOMATIC CHOKE CONTROL.

a. General. The automatic choke is controlled by heat from the engine. The engine must be cold to adjust a choke of this type. Two general designs are commonly used. One has the heating unit mounted on the exhaust manifold, with the choke lever controlled by a short rod attached to an arm on the thermostatic control (fig 50). The second type, which is circular, is attached to the upper part of the carburetor body (fig 51}. The cover is marked with graduations and pointer and has a mark at the center for a neutral setting. An arrow on the face of the cover indicates the direction in which the cover should be turned from center position to obtain a leaner or richer mixture. .

b. Electric-choke adjustment. Remove the air cleaner, and set the hand throttle to quarter-open position to release the fast idle cam. Move the choke lever until the hole in the shaft alines with the slot in the bearing boss (fig 50, inset). Insert a nail in the hole through the slot until it engages the notch in the flanged base of the thermostat housing. Loosen the clamp bolt on the automatic-choke lever, and push the lever up until the choke butterfly is tightly closed (fig 50). Hold the lever in this position, and tighten the bolt clamping the choke lever to the shaft. Remove the nail from the hole and slot. Test the action to be certain that the choke valve does not bind or stick. The Idle mechanism and the choke should be free of any gum or carbon deposits. Install the air cleaner. Always test the adjustment with the throttle partly open.

c. Climatic-choke adjustment. Before adjusting the climatic control, be certain that the screen in the thermostat housing is not obstructed. Remove the housing screws (fig 51a) and the cover with care so that the tongue on the thermostat coil releases from the choke valve shaft lever as the cover is separated from the carburetor body. Remove and clean the screen (fig 51b). Replace the screen and install the thermostat-coil housing or cover with the marks down. Insert the housing screws and retainers. Turn the housing counterclockwise until the pointer and housing marks show neutral. Adjust to two notches rich. In this position the choke should close and seat in the air intake assembly and move to full open position as the engine warms up and reaches operating temperature. Should it fall to do so, loosen the housing screws and rotate the housing one mark at a time until the desired action is obtained. This adjustment will create a lean or rich air-fuel mixture to meet the demands of the atmospheric temperature.

d. Replacement. When the automatic choke is mounted on the carburetor, the carburetor and the choke can be replaced only as a single unit. As a rule, this is the climatic type. The electric type is mounted independently on the exhaust manifold with screws (fig 50) and can be removed from the manifold by disconnecting the wire, releasing the choke control rod, and removing the mounting screws. Select a duplicate of the old choke; slide the control arm on the shaft of the new choke, and set the unit In place on the manifold. Install the screws and the choke-valve control rod. When connecting the wire be careful not to over tighten the screw as this may break the insulator. Adjust the choke valve.

57. CARBURETOR IDLE ADJUSTMENT.
a. The only adjustment of fuel mixture which can be made by the second and third echelons is the idle adjustment. To correct local conditions, the idle adjustment must be changed. The double-barrel type of carburetor is equipped with dual idling-adjustment screws, and an adjustment must be made on both screws while the engine is running at normal operating temperature.

b. Set the throttle stop screw on the carburetor to operate the engine at approximately 400 to 500rpm. This setting should drive an unloaded vehicle between 5 and 8 mph on a smooth road.

c. Locate and turn the adjustment screw in until it seats (fig 52). Forcing this screw will break the needle. Turn the screw out 1/2 to 1-1/2 turns, depending on the size of the carburetor, and start the engine. Turn the adjusting screw in or out, 1/8th of a turn at a time, until a smooth idle is obtained. If a vacuum gage is available, connect the tube to a vacuum adapter on the intake manifold (windshield wiper) and turn the adjusting screw until the highest vacuum is reached with smooth operation.

58. CARBURETOR REMOVAL.
a. Controls. Loosen the clamp screw, and remove or disconnect the air cleaner. Disconnect the choke and remove the throttle and accelerator controls. Disconnect the fuel line and vacuum spark-advance control line to prevent any damage to them. It may be necessary to loosen all carburetor flange

nuts and loosen the carburetor before removing the nuts.

b. Removal. Handle the carburetor carefully, always holding it in an upright position. Do not allow it to tilt, for this would cause any accumulation of sediment in the fuel bowl to become agitated and to enter and clog the jet openings. Never place the carburetor in a location where dirt can enter the connection to which the fuel line attaches. If the flange is to be replaced, remove it to a safe place.

59. CARBURETOR INSTALLATION.

a. Replacement. When the carbu-

retor used is a replacement, be certain that it is identical in size, shape, and model number with the one removed. The mounting flange must be the same; the fuel connections must match; the throttle lever, the choke control and an connections must be identical Be certain all gaskets, are in good condition. If the carburetor has a governor, any ports cut through the gasket must aline with the governor flange and match the holes in the carburetor. Start all the flange nuts before tightening any particular one, and draw them all down evenly.

Caution: **Tightening one flange**

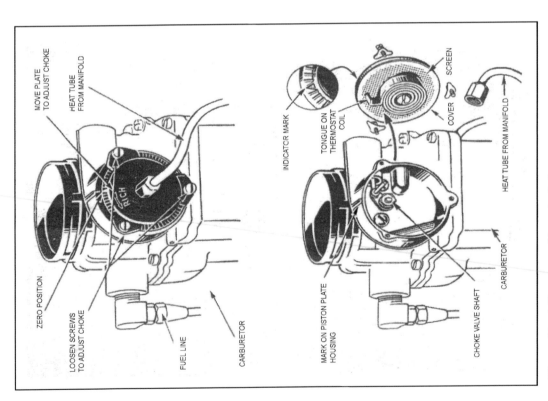

Figure 51. Adjustment of hot-air choke

nut or bolt before tightening the others may result in a flange being broken or cracked.

b. Controls. Connect and adjust the throttle control. Connect the fuel line and tighten the union nuts. Two wrenches should be use d to tighten the union nuts so the fittings will escape any damage. Connect the vacuum spark-advance control line if there is one.

c. Adjustment. Before attempting to start the engine, pump the carburetor bowl full of fuel. Use the hand operated priming lever located on the fuel pump, or, if the engine is not so equipped, crank the engine with the cranking motor, leaving the ignition turned off. Adjust the screw in the carburetor throttle-stop bracket to control the idling speed. Adjust the choke valve while the engine is cold, and inspect this valve when the engine has reached normal operating temperature. Install the air cleaner. The carburetor idle mixture should be set at this time.

60. GOVERNOR.

The governor is not an actual part of the fuel system, but it affects engine performance by regulating the fuel as necessary to limit the engine to a set maximum speed. A vacuum or velocity-operated governor is mounted between the carburetor

and the intake manifold and will fail to operate properly when its parts become worn. If the moving parts appear to be clogged, they should be cleaned with solvent. Replace the governor if it does not operate properly.

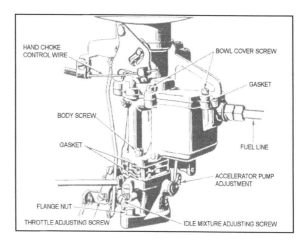

Figure 52. Carburetor adjustment

73

61. TROUBLE SHOOTING.

If the fuel pump is not operating properly, the engine will not operate. Trouble can be quickly isolated in the fuel pump by determining whether fuel is reaching the pump from the fuel tank and being pumped into the line leading to the carburetor. If the fuel pump is found to be defective, proceed to inspect the pump itself.

62. TYPES.

Fuel pumps are of two basic types; electrical and mechanical.

a. Mechanical. The location and construction of mechanical fuel pumps vary widely with the types of engines used, but the methods of inspection and replacement are essentially the same for all types. In one type (fig 53) a cam on the camshaft engages directly with the face or the rocker arm of the fuel pump. A second type (fig 54) has a fixed or adjustable push rod which is actuated by the camshaft and in turn moves the pump rocker arm. A third type (fig 55) has a fixed or adjustable push rod driven from a cam on the distributor shaft.

b. Electric. The electric fuel pump (fig 56) has a bellows-type diaphragm connected to the armature of a solenoid motor. As the ignition switch is turned on, the spring-loaded armature is energized and moves against the spring until the circuit is broken and the spring returns the armature to the original, position. This creates the reciprocating action of the pump.

63. MECHANICAL FUEL PUMP.

a. Inspection. First examine the sediment bowl for dirt or water. A glass bowl can be inspected without removal but a metal bowl must be removed for inspection. If necessary, remove: the sediment bowl and clean it thoroughly; wash the screen with cleaning fluid and blow It out with compressed air. Use a new gasket when installing the bowl, for' the pump will not operate with an air leak at this point. This operation must be performed more often during freezing weather, for ice in the bowl will stop the flow of fuel. Inspect the fuel connections for any leaks indicated by fuel seeping or dripping from joints, and tighten the connections if necessary. If tightening the top cover screws fails to stop a leak at that point, install a new gasket.

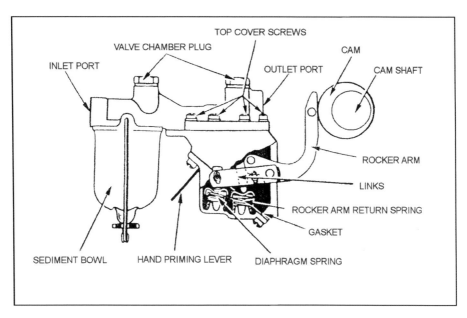

Figure 53. Mechanical fuel pump operated by the camshaft

b. Test procedure. To test the pump, be sure that there is fuel in the tank and that the:fuel shut-off valve is open. Disconnect the fuel line at the carburetor inlet If the connection is an elbow and not a straight adapter, use a pair of pliers to hold the elbow. Test, the pump by operating the hand priming lever or by cranking the engine with the cranking motor (ignition off). If the engine is stopped so that dia-phragm is held in the extended po-sition, it will be necessary to crank the engine before the hand priming lever win work. If fuel is reaching the pump but not being pumped out the end of the fuel line, replace the pump.

c. Removal. Close the fuel shut-off valve. Disconnect the fuel lines at the pump, using two wrenches to avoid any damage to the fittings. Clean the dirt and grease from the base of the fuel pump at the point where it is fastened to the engine. Remove the mounting screws and the pump and gasket. If the pump is driven by a push rod, remove the rod for cleaning and inspection.

d. Installation. Be sure to use a pump of proper size, type, and model. Connections and air breather must be clean and free from dirt. Remove any dust caps or plugs from the connections. Place a new gasket on the fuel-pump mounting, holding it in place with gasket seal or grease. Spacers can used to restore pump-line pressure.

75

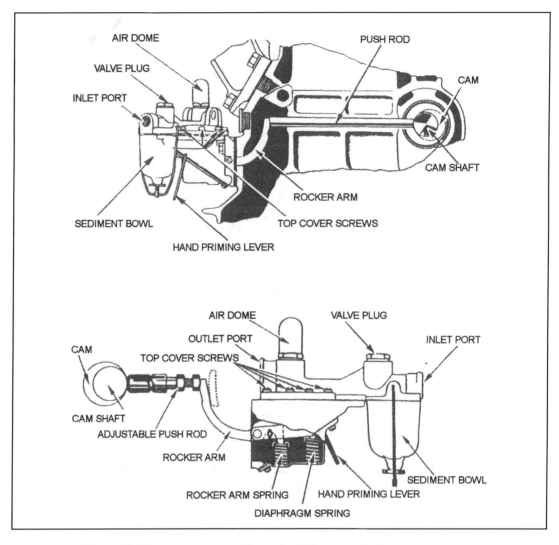

Figure 54. Fuel pump operated by pushrod from camshaft

Insert the fuel-pump rocker arm through the opening in the case or against the plunger. Hold the pump in position and tighten the nuts or capscrews. Start the union nuts of the fittings by hand and then tighten them with wrenches. This will avoid any damage due to cross threading. Open the fuel shut off valve. Prime the pump with the hand priming lever, or operate the cranking motor. Start the engine and inspect the pump and connections for fuel leaks.

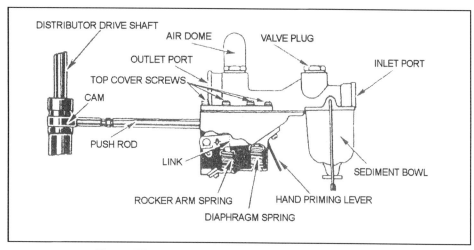

Figure 55. Mechanical fuel pump driven by distributor shaft

64. ELECTRIC FUEL PUMP.

a. Inspection. Examine the terminals on both ends of the cable leading from the ignition switch to the pump. They must be clean, tight, and well soldered to the cable. The cable must be free of breaks, and the insulation should be in good condition. The pump must be well grounded at the mounting, especially if the fuel lines are connected with flexible hose. Inspect the fuel connections for leakage. Remove the filter screen and wash it in solvent. Use a new gasket when replacing the cover for the pump will not work if there is an air leak at this point.

b. Test procedure. The ignition switch controls the supply of current to the electric fuel pump, but an automatic shut-off switch within the pump itself cuts off 'the pump when the ignition switch is on and the engine not running. This shut-off switch is controlled by pressure in the fuel line to the carburetor so that the pump will not operate when the carburetor float bowl is full. Therefore, do not assume that the pump must be defective just because it does not operate when the switch is turned on. To relieve pressure in the fuel line when testing the pump, it is preferable to try to start the engine rather than disconnect the fuel line at one of the units. If the pump fails to operate, test the electrical circuit by removing the cable from the terminal post of the pump, moving it well away from the pump, and striking it against a ground. A light flash (ignition switch on) indicates that the circuit is complete and the pump is defective. Never strike the cable close to the pump, for a fire might be started if there happened

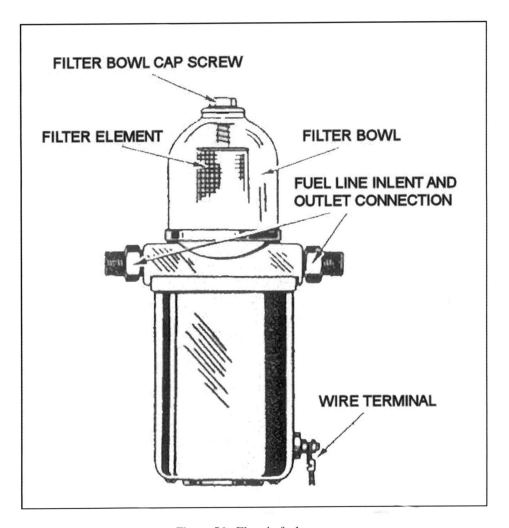

Figure 56. Electric fuel pump

to be a fuel leak at or near the pump.

c. Removal. Turn the ignition switch off and close the fuel shutoff valve. Disconnect the cable from the binding post on the fuel pump, and disconnect the fuel-line fittings, using two wrenches to avoid any damage. Remove the bolts holding the pump to the frame or bracket.

d. Installation. Select a pump of the same size, type, and voltage as the one removed. The inlet and outlet openings must be free from dirt. If the new pump does not have fuel connections, transfer the connections from the old pump. Make certain that the face of the pump and the frame or mounting bracket are clean so the ground circuit will be completed. Install the pump and tighten the mounting bolts. Attach the cable, install and tighten the fuel connections, and test the pump.

65. VACUUM PUMP.

a. General. Not all vehicles are equipped with a vacuum pump. The primary purpose of such a pump is to provide a vacuum for the operation of the windshield wipers when the engine is accelerating or operating under a load and the manifold vacuum has reduced to a point where it will not operate the wiper motor. Ordinarily this pump is of the diaphragm type, and is an integral part of the fuel pump housing. It is powered by linkage from the fuel pump and lubricated from the engine crankcase.

b. Inspection. On vehicles equipped with the vacuum pump, the windshield wipers should function at an approximately constant speed at all times. Failure or sluggish operation indicates a leak in the vacuum system or the intake manifold. Examine all the lines and connections for leaks. Remove both lines from the pump housing, and operate the engine. A definite vacuum should be noted at one connection and a slight pressure at the other. A broken or cracked diaphragm in the pump housing will be indicated by a weak vacuum and practically no pressure. If the vacuum pump Is mounted below the fuel pump, a defective diaphragm will also be indicated by excessive oil consumption. When this condition prevails, the pump should be replaced as an assembly.

c. Removal. To remove a fuel and vacuum pump unit, close the fuel shut-off cock, disconnect all lines to the pump, and remove the mounting screws. It may be necessary to turn the unit to withdraw the actuating arm.

d. Installation. To install the unit place the actuating arm through a new gasket and position the pump on the engine. Start the mounting screws and tighten them evenly. Connect the fuel and vacuum lines and turn the shut-off cock to "on." Start the engine, and, inspect the connections for leakage. Test the windshield-wiper action.

66. TROUBLE SHOOTING.

The fuel filter is not likely to become so badly clogged that it restricts the flow of fuel to the engine. If it is filled with dirt and water, it may fail to filter the fuel properly, allowing dirty fuel to pass through to the carburetor and clog the jets. On certain vehicles, small secondary filters, usually mounted on the carbu-retor, may become so clogged that they shut off the flow of fuel to the carburetor entirely. These must then be thoroughly cleaned.

67. INSPECTION.

Close the fuel shut-off valve and remove the drain plug (figs 57, 58) to empty the filter. If there's a no-

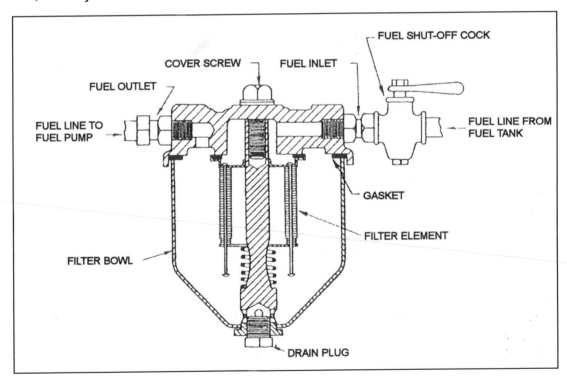

Figure 57. Fuel filter with spring-held element

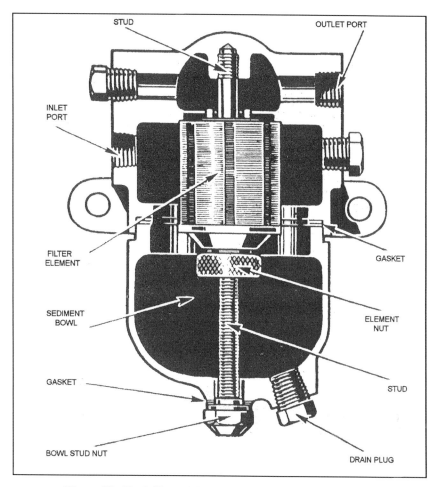

Figure 58. Fuel filter with element held by knurled nut

ticeable amount of dirt or water present, clean the filter. If the fuel filter is below the level of the fuel tank, open the shut-off valve for a few seconds and allow the fuel to drain through the filter to flush the line.

68. CLEANING.
Remove the filter bowl and element. Wash the filter element in cleaning fluid and clean with a soft brush. Do not use compressed air under high pressure, for the filter element is fragile and will be damaged. Replace any gaskets that are damaged or hardened. If the filter is held in place with a knurled nut, tighten it finger tight. After assembly, open the fuel shut-off valve, start the engine, and inspect carefully for leaks around the gasket or drain plug.

69. TROUBLE SHOOTING.

The most common malfunction of the fuel tank is *emptiness* - a condition that is easily remedied. If the engine fails to start, always check to see that there is fuel in the tank before making any other test. The procedure for checking a defective fuel gage is given in paragraph 75.

70. TANK INSPECTION.

Examine the anchor bands or straps that secure the tank to the carrier or brackets. They should be free from cracks or breaks. If there is insulation between the straps and the tank to prevent wear, see that this insulation is in place and tighten the straps. Inspect the tank for signs of wear and leaks, especially around the brackets. Dampness indicates that a slight leak may be present. Inspect the filler neck; it should be tightly soldered or riveted to the tank and should not leak at the joint.

71. VENT OPENING.

If the vent opening is in the filler cap, it may be a simple opening or a pressure-type vent. In the pressure type (fig 59), be sure that both valves operate. The vent may be located inside the filler tube or at the fuel-gage housing. In any case the vent must be in good working order for fuel to flow.

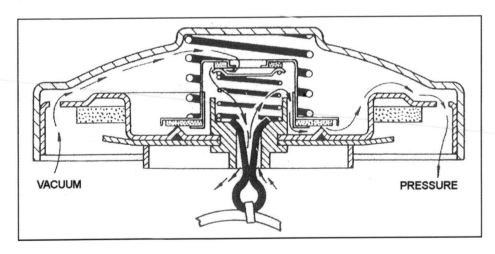

VACUUM

PRESSURE

Figure 59. Fuel-tank filler cap

72. WATER IN TANK.

Water may accumulate in the tank from the condensation of moisture. The best way to. avoid this is to keep the tank filled with fuel. To remove the water, open the tank drain plug; the water will be at the bottom of the tank and will drain out first. Drain until the fuel pouring from the drain plug is free of water, or, if there is time, drain the tank completely. Catch the fuel in a container. The water can be separated from the fuel by straining through filter paper or chamois. *Caution: Gasoline flowing over a surface generates static electricity that will result in a spark unless the surface is grounded. Provide a metallic contact between the container and the tank.*

Editors' Note: Straining the fuel is not very practical (even when prices seemingly shot sky high!). I suggest that you use a fuel drying additive. If you drain the water/gasoline, please dispose of safely and responsibly.

73. COLD-WEATHER OPERATION.

Water in the gasoline will freeze in cold weather, and ice crystals will clog the fuel lines and carburetor jets. To prevent this when operating in low temperatures, add 1 quart of denatured alcohol, grade 3, to the fuel tank at the start of the winter season and 1 pint per month thereafter.

74. TANK REPAIRS.

Do not try to repair leaks in fuel tanks by soldering. *Even though the tank has been drained and washed, an explosive mixture of fuel and air is likely to remain in the tank and any attempt to apply a flame to the exterior will result in a serious accident.* Any fuel tank that leaks should be replaced.

Editors' note: Throwing away your fuel tank because it leaks may not be an option. There are a number of products on the market that will let you line your tank and make it good as new. One product that I have used with success is offered by J.C. Whitney™. It is a 1-qt. can of "Alcohol-resistant Gas Tank Sealer." Just be sure to follow the directions and remove the fuel gage, etc. Be sure that the pick up fuel line doesn't become clogged by apply a slight air pressure to the line.

75. FUEL GAGE TEST.

To simplify testing of the fuel gage, it is recommended that the test be made with the tank approximately half full so the gage will not normally read "full" or "empty."

a. If gage is dead. If the gage is

dead (that is, needle remains to left of empty) when the ignition switch is turned on, the current is not reaching the gage. To test, connect a jumper wire from the ignition terminal to the gage to. either terminal of the ignition switch. If the gage registers, the wire from the ignition switch to the gage must be defective.

b. If gage is stuck. If the gage remains in anyone position (other than dead) as the ignition switch is turned on and off, the gage is defective or the tank-unit float is stuck. To determine which is at fault, ground the tank-unit terminal with a jumper wire or screw driver. If the gage shows empty, replace the tank unit; if the gage does not move, replace gage.

c. If gage registers incorrectly. If the gage registers when the ignition switch is turned an but is known to register incorrectly, the tank-unit float arm is bent or distorted and the tank unit must be replaced.

d. If gage registers empty. If the gage registers empty when the ignition switch is turned on, the wire from the gage to the tank is shorted and must be repaired or replaced.

e. If gage registers full. If the gage registers full when: the ignition switch is turned on, either the wire from the gage to the tank unit is broken or the tank unit itself is defective. To determine which is at fault, ground the tank unit terminal with a jumper wire or screw driver. If the gage then shows empty, replace the tank unit; if the gage still shows full, repair or replace the gage-to-tank-unit wire.

76. TROUBLE SHOOTING.

If a fuel line is clogged or broken, the engine will not operate. A broken fuel line may be readily located visually. A clogged line can be located by following the procedure outlined in Chapter 2.

77. INSPECTION.

Examine all fuel lines for cracks, dents, or wear. Notice particularly those points where moving parts are located or where a shift of vehicle load might damage the lines. Fuel lines should never rub against

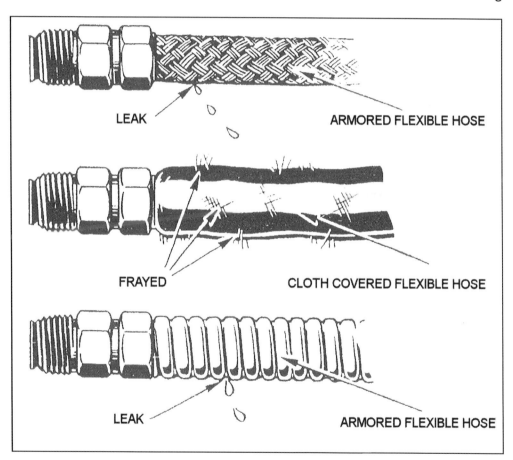

Figure 60. Fuel leaks at flexible hose

the frame or strike any sharp metal edge. Do not bend or change the shape of a sweated-steel line; this could very easily break open the seam.

78. FLEXIBLE HOSE.
If flexible hose is used to connect a unit to the fuel line, examine it for cracks or seepage (fig 60). Replace it with a new hose whenever such damage is evident. The hose must be long enough to sag when connected so it can flex with every movement between units.

Editors' Note: Do not use copper

tubing for fuel lines. Copper is a soft metal and will crack under the stress of vibrations.

79. CONNECTIONS.
When the connections (fig 61) are in two pieces (a connector that screws into the unit and a coupling nut that is screwed on the connector) use two wrenches for loosening or removing the nut. When installing a coupling nut to a fuel connection start it by hand and turn finger tight; then complete the tightening with a wrench. To tighten a fitting, use two wrenches. First loosen the coupling nut; then tighten the con-

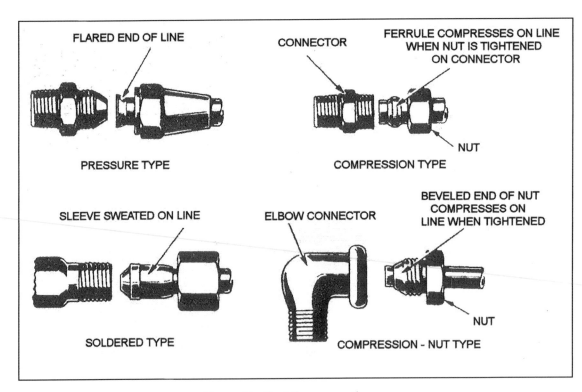

Figure 61. Fuel-line connections

nector; and finally retighten the coupling nut. This procedure prevents twisting the fuel line.

80. LINE REPAIR.

a. Plain end. Replacement of a broken line is not always necessary. If the line is broken at a point near a connection, the line can be repaired if a strain is not created by the shorter length. Slide the coupling nut away from the end; remove the damaged portion of the line; and dress the end of the line with a file. Clean the fillings from the line and apply a new sealing member. This may be a ferrule, a ferrule and nut combine, or a nut that compresses against the line when under tension.

b. Flared fittings. To repair a flared fitting, cut off the damaged flare (fig 62) and dress the end of the line to remove the ragged edges. Clean away the filings and place the line in the flaring tool so that the tube is flush with the top of the die. Tighten the clamp holding the tubing in the die, and place some lubricating oil on the end of the tube. Use the flaring tool by sliding the cone-shaped compressor over the holding tool and turning the handle until the proper-sized flare is formed. A thorough inspection of the flare should be made for cracks upon completion.

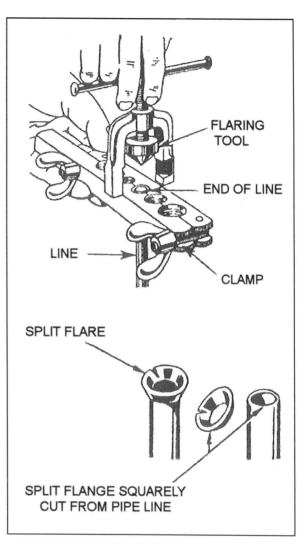

Figure 62.   Flaring the end of a copper line—
*Editors' Note: **Do NOT use copper for fuel or brake lines. Copper is too brittle a metal.***

SECTION VII INTAKE MANIFOLD

81. TROUBLE SHOOTING.
Leaks in the intake manifold will cause a low vacuum, which will mean a loss of engine power. Inspect the manifold for leaks as outlined below; also check the windshield wiper, governor, and carburetor for leaks.

82. INSPECTION.
a. Oil test. With the engine idling, spread oil from the spout of an oil can along the gasket edges. If there is a leak around the gasket, oil will be drawn through and a heavy blue smoke will come out of the exhaust pipe. If this occurs, tighten the nuts or cap screws holding the intake manifold and repeat the test. If this does not stop the leaks, replace the gasket.

b. Vacuum gage test. If a vacuum gage is available, use it to test the intake manifold. Connect the gage to the windshield wiper connection on the intake manifold and operate the engine with the cranking motor (ignition off). The needle should rise sharply to approximately 15 to 20 in.

of vacuum. It should hold this reading for a few seconds after the cranking motor is disengaged and then drop slowly to 0. If the manifold is leaking, the needle will have a much lower reading and will drop quickly to 0 when the cranking motor is disengaged.

83. WINDSHIELD WIPER.
a. General. The windshield wiper operates from the vacuum created in the intake manifold. When the speed of the engine increases or the engine operates at full throttle, the vacuum in the manifold will decrease. Unless a vacuum booster pump is used, the windshield wiper will slow down or stop at full throttle. Tests must be made with the engine idling. Two pieces of metal tubing, connected by a rubber tube, connect the windshield wiper to the manifold. The rubber tube provides for flexibility between engine and cab.

b. Inspection. A leak in the windshield-wiper line can usually be detected by a hissing sound. Test or

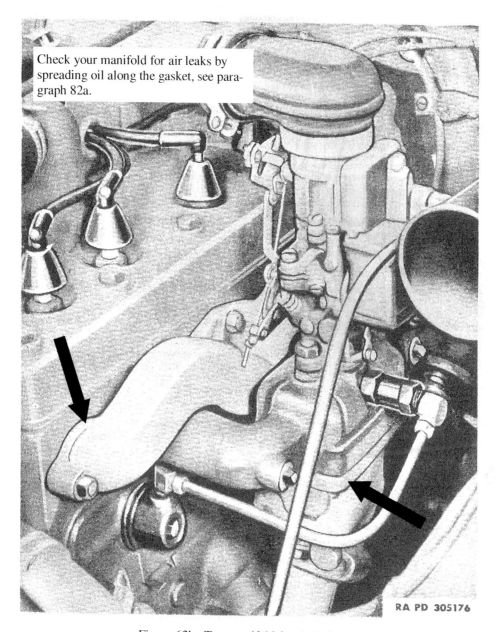

Check your manifold for air leaks by spreading oil along the gasket, see paragraph 82a.

RA PD 305176

Figure 62b. Test manifold for air leaks

leaks by use of oil in the same manner as the intake manifold gasket test (par 82a). Replace any broken or rotted rubber tubing. If the metal tube is defective, it may be necessary to remove some of the interior trim in order to gain access to the tube.

84. TROUBLE SHOOTING.

Leaks in the exhaust system can be detected by a sharp spitting noise made by the escaping gas when the engine is suddenly accelerated. Exhaust gases are poisonous, and all leaks should be corrected immediately. Leaks are especially dangerous in winter when the cab is likely to be tightly closed. If the exhaust passages are restricted, a back pressure will build up that will result in lack of power and failure to idle, and which may cause the engine to die. Accelerate the engine to high speed and then reduce to an idle. A hissing sound will indicate that there is a restriction in the exhaust system.

85. EXHAUST MANIFOLD.

Inspect the nuts or cap screws that hold the manifold to the engine and those that hold the exhaust-pipe flange to the manifold. If the gaskets are blown out, they should be replaced. Overheating may warp the manifold enough to cause binding between the mounting studs and holes or at the

manifold clamps. If this condition occurs, the manifold may leak around the gaskets and become extremely difficult to tighten properly. It is advisable to remove the manifold and grind down the surfaces where interference occurs. This may save many hours of labor in replacing gaskets damaged by manifold distortion.

86. HEAT CONTROL VALVE.

A portion of the exhaust gas is diverted to a hot spot in the intake manifold or to a passage surrounding the point where the fuel enters the intake manifold. This heat helps

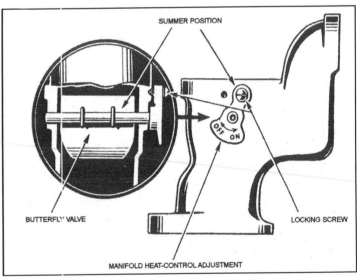

Figure 63. Manually adjusted manifold heat control

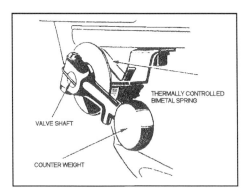

Figure 64. Automatic manifold heat control

vaporize the fuel and is controlled by a valve which may be either manually (fig 63) or thermally (fig 64) controlled. The shaft that holds the valve butterfly must turn freely in a thermally controlled valve so the bimetal spring can move the valve to a closed position as the manifold temperature increases. If heat has caused the shaft to scale and stick, apply penetrating oil or a solution of washing soda In kerosene. Do not use common engine oil, for the heat of the manifold will cause the oil to carbonize and form a sticky gum on the valve. If this does not free the shaft, remove the unit and clean the shaft with fine sandpaper or emery cloth. Inspect the spring on the thermally operated type to be certain that it is resting in its proper position on the stop located on the exhaust manifold.

87. MUFFLER.
Exhaust gases may condense in the muffler and hasten rusting of the metal walls. If a part of the muffler has rusted or blown through, an emergency repair may be made by wrapping a piece of sheet iron around that part and fastening it with wire or by brazing with an oxyacetylene torch. The muffler should have a small hole (about 1/8 in) in the lowest section of its outside shell to permit condensation to drain out,

88. TAIL PIPE.
The exhaust pipe leading from the muffler to the rear of the vehicle may become crushed in or obstructed with mud so that the flow of exhaust gas is sharply restricted. Inspect to see that it is open. If there is a hissing sound when the engine is dropped from high speed to a slow idle, examine the tail pipe carefully.

CHAPTER 5

COOLING SYSTEM

89. TROUBLE SHOOTING.

The most logical place to look for the cause of an overheated engine is in the cooling system. However, lack of oil in the crankcase or late ignition timing will also cause overheating, even though the cooling system is functioning properly. *Check these possible causes before making extensive tests of the cooling system.*

a. Overheating. Lack of liquid in the cooling system is the most common cause of engine overheating. The liquid can be lost either by leaking from the cooling system or by boiling. Determine which is the cause.

[1] Leakage. Carefully check the radiator hose connections, water-pump mounting bolts, seal and gasket, thermostat mounting bolts and gasket, and the cylinder-head bolts and gasket. Make any repairs nec-essary to eliminate leakage. Inspect the radiator core for leakage. The leak may be internal, caused by a cracked cylinder head or block or a defective cylinder-head gasket. Such leakage would be evidenced by bubbles or foam on the oil dip stick or by a raised oil level in the crankcase. If this evidence is found, either replace the cylinder head or gasket or remove the engine for repairs.

[2] Boiling. The most likely cause of the liquid's boiling is a loose or broken fan belt. Clogged air passages in the radiator core will have the same effect. If the thermostat is stuck closed, the liquid in the engine block and cylinder head will heat excessively; this condition of the thermostat will be indicated by a high reading on the temperature gage when the radiator core is comparatively cool. In temperatures below freezing, boiling may indicate that the coolant is frozen in the radiator core and therefore unable to circulate. If air or exhaust gas is getting into the system, the engine parts will rust rapidly and this will eventually clog the small water passages in the radiator core. If the radiator is clogged, it should be flushed out. (Par 4)

b. Overcooling. Overcooling is caused by the thermostat being stuck open. This is indicated by the fact that the engine does not warm up to the proper operating temperature. Remove the thermostat and inspect it.

90. DRAINING.

Remove the radiator filler cap, and open the radiator drain cock. Also open the drain cock at the bottom of the cylinder block (usually at the left rear). If the cooling liquid contains antifreeze solution, collect the liquid in suitable containers. If the vehicle has a hot-water heater, be sure to drain it by removing the bottom heater hose. If the cooling system is not refilled immediately, attach a tag marked "*No water in cooling system*" to the steering wheel.

Editors' Note: Be sure to dispose of used antifreeze solutions in a safe manner. It can be an extremely dangerous substance to animals and children.

91. REFILLING.

Close the radiator and cylinder-block drain cocks. Fill the system through the radiator filler neck until cooling liquid can be seen. Use clean, soft water. Avoid water containing alkali or other substances that promote the accumulation of scale and rust. It is desirable that the water not be too cold, for cold water causes the thermostat to close and this may trap air in the cylinder block or head. Any air trapped in this way would slowly leak out through the bleeder hole in the thermostat, lowering water level in the radiator. *Always check the water level after the engine is warmed up, and add water if necessary*. Install radiator cap, being certain to turn it all the way to the locked position.

92. CLEANING AND FLUSHING.

a. With water hose. Dirty water can be flushed out of the cooling system if a hose and water supply are available (fig 65). Remove the lower radiator hose. Remove the thermostat, and replace the thermostat housing. Place the end of the water hose in the lower hose of the radiator, and wrap cloth around the connection to preserve some of the pressure. Allow water to run through the radiator in the reverse direction of normal flow until it runs clean. Then move the hose to the thermostat housing and flush the engine water jacket until it too is perfectly clean. Replace the thermostat and the radiator hose.

b. With cleaning compound.

The cooling system should be given a thorough cleaning if it becomes clogged with rust or other deposits. In localities where water contains dissolved salts, cleaning will be necessary more often than under normal conditions. Twice a year is usually desirable, as well as before and alter using antifreeze solution. Issue cleaning compound (Federal Stock Number 51-C-1568-500) is recommended. It consists of an active cleaning agent and a neutralizer. Any good commercial cleaner can be used.

[1] Drain the system and remove the thermostat. Replace the thermostat housing and top hose. Fill the system, and run the engine until it reaches operating temperature. Stop the engine and drain the system. This will remove loose rust.

[2] Close the drain cocks and pour the required quantity of cleaner in the system. Fill with clean water.

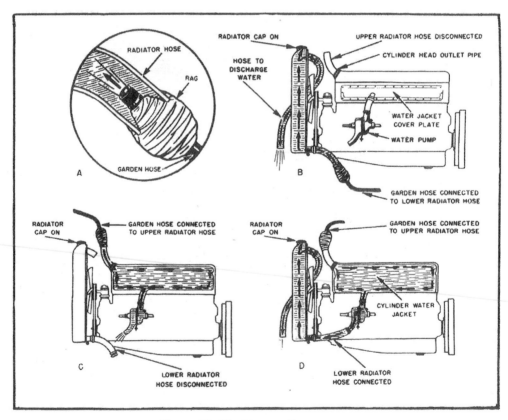

Figure 65. Flushing cooling system

Run the engine until the temperature reaches 180°F (cover the radiator if necessary) and then continue to run the engine for 30 minutes. Do not allow the solution to boil and do not drive the vehicle. Stop the engine and drain the system.

[3] Close the drain cocks and pour the neutralizer into the system. Fill with clean water, and run the engine until it reaches operating temperature. Stop the engine and drain the system.

c. With flushing gun. If a combination water and air-pressure flushing gun is available, the cooling system should be flushed out after the cleaning compound is used. Be sure the thermostat is removed, and replace the pressure cap with a sealing cap.

[1] Remove both upper and lower radiator hoses. Install a 3-ft length of hose on both the radiator inlet and outlet. The hose attached to the upper radiator connection should be placed so the water will flow out of the engine compartment.

[2] Connect the flushing gun to the hose at the lower radiator connection. Turn on the water until the radiator is full, then apply air pressure gradually to avoid any damage to the radiator. Shut off the air, fill the radiator with water, and apply air pressure again. Repeat this procedure there or four times.

[3] Connect the flushing gun to the hose at the upper radiator connection. Repeat the flushing operation until the water runs clear.

[4] Connect the sections of hose to the thermostat housing and the water-pump housing, and flush the engine water jacket in the same manner.

93. RUST PREVENTIVE.
The use of an inhibitor or rust preventive reduces or prevents corrosion in the cooling system. It is advisable to add an inhibitor to the water after cleaning and flushing. Antifreeze usually contains an inhibitor, so when antifreeze is used with the coolant no additional inhibitor is necessary. The inhibitor will "wear out" after a year or two and should be replaced at least annually with either new radiator fluid or an inhibitor additive.

94. TEST FOR AIR AND EXHAUST.
Air or exhaust leaking into the cooling system and circulating through it will cause rapid corrosion. Air may get in as a result of a low level of liquid in the radiator, a leaky water pump, or loose connections. Exhaust gases may be blown past the

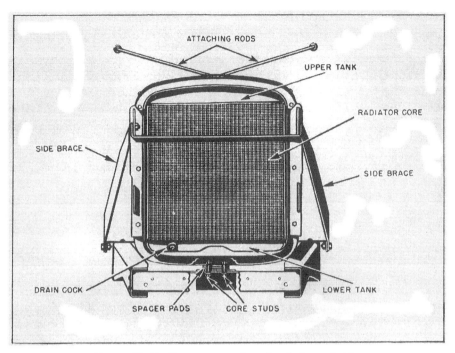

Figure 66. Radiator mounted anchor bolts and shims

cylinderhead gasket or through cracks in the cylinder head and block.

a. Air - suction test. Adjust the level of the cooling liquid to avoid any overflow loss during the test. Tighten the radiator cap until it is airtight. Attach a length of rubber tube to the overflow tube, making the connection airtight. Run the engine at a fast idle until the temperature gage reaches operating temperature. Without changing the engine speed, place the end of the rubber tube in a bottle of water. A void any kinks or bends in the rubber tube. If bubbles of air appear continuously in the bottle of water, air is being sucked into the cooling system.

b. Exhaust - gas test. Start the test with the engine cold. Remove the fan belt so the water pump will not operate. Drain the cooling system below thermostat level, and remove the thermostat. Fill the engine water jacket until the thermostat housing is full of water. Start the engine and "gun" it several times. Bubbles in the water in the thermostat housing indicate that exhaust gas is leaking into the cooling system. Make the test quickly before the water starts to boil. If there is any leakage, replace the cylinderhead gasket and check the head

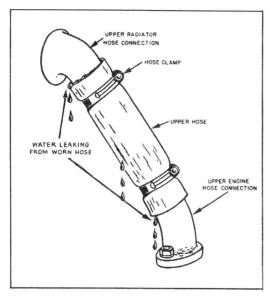

Figure 67. Damaged radiator water hose

and block for cracks.

95. RADIATOR.

a. Inspection. Examine the radiator (fig 66) for leaks. Leaks may occur where the drain cock or plug enters the lower tank, at the outlet pipe, where the upper and lower tanks are attached to the core at the tank seams, or in the water cells of the core. Inspect the core for insects, paper, dirt, or leaves which may be clogging the air passages. Inspect the anchor bolts and support rods, and tighten them if necessary.

b. Cleaning. If the air passages are clogged, wet the outside surface of the radiator core until all foreign matter is saturated. Then direct a stream of water from the engine side through the air passages of the core until the air passages are free. An ordinary garden hose can be used to supply the stream of water. Straighten any segregator plates that may be bent so that they restrict the air passages.

96. WATER HOSE.

a. Inspection. Examine the hose (fig 67) for broken or oil-soaked outer covering and exposed fabric.

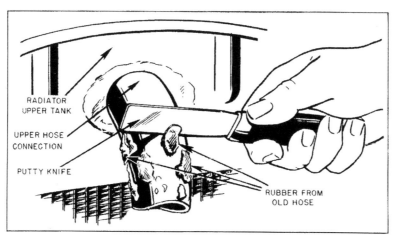

Figure 68. Cleaning water outlets for installation of new hose.

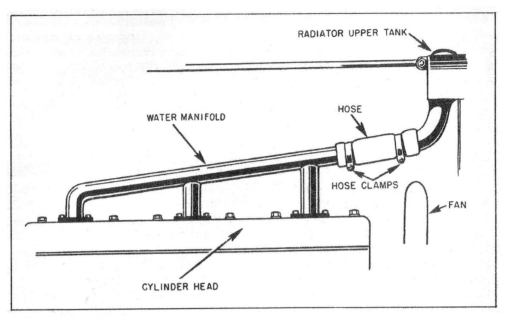

Figure 69. Cooling-system manifold on cylinder head

Compress the hose at a point midway between the connections. Any hose that has become spongy should be replaced. Look for leaks around the clamp screws. If there are any leaks, tighten the clamp screws and inspect again before rejecting the hose.

b. Replacement. Drain the cooling system. Loosen the clamp screws and clamps. Twist the hose free of the connections, and scrape the pipe connections clean (fig 68). Install a section of hose the same diameter and length, positioning the clamp screws for easy tightening. Be sure the pipe connections enter the hose far enough to be caught by the clamp screws. Tighten the

clamp screws, and fill the cooling system.

97. WATER PIPE.
Some vehicles have a manifold (fig (69) to convey the coolant from the engine water jacket to the radiator. On other vehicles a by-pass pipe may connect the rear of the cylinder head with the water pump or with the radiator. If this part is attached by mounting flanges, inspect the bolts or nuts and the gaskets; if attached by threaded connections, inspect for leaks around the connections.

98. WATER PUMP.
a. Inspection. Examine the mounting bolts or nuts to see that

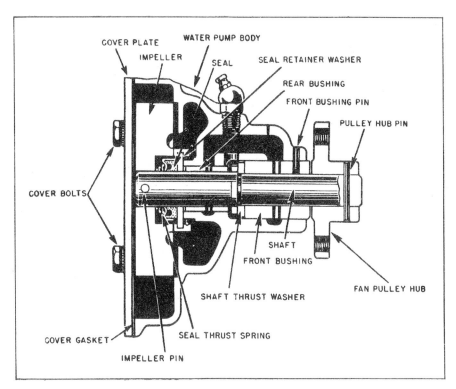

Figure 70. Water pump with internal water seal

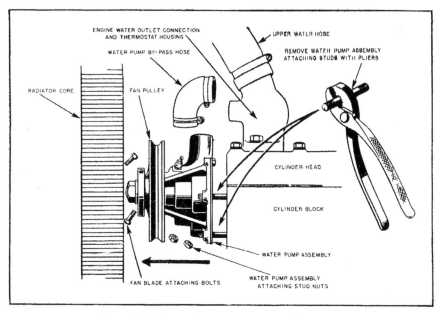

Figure 71. Removing water pump studs

99

the pump is tightly mounted. Look for water leaks around the shaft. If leaks are found in a pump that uses a packing gland, tighten the packing nut. Do not tighten more than necessary to stop the leak. If the nut turns to the limit of adjustment without stopping the leak, repack the pump. If a leak occurs in a pump with a nonadjustable seal, (fig 70), replace the pump.

b. Removal.
[1] Front mounted pump. First drain the cooling system. Then remove the fan belt. Loosen the hose clamps, and remove the hose. Remove the fan. Remove the attaching stud nuts, and move the pump toward the radiator until the studs clear the holes. Then remove the pump from the vehicle. If the space is not sufficient to allow the pump to clear the studs, move it as far as possible. Then unscrew the studs with a pipe wrench or a pair of pliers (fig 71).

Editors' Note: I suggest using a stud puller or the old fashioned puller of jamming two nuts together and then using a wrench to "pull" the stud.

[2] Shaft - driven pump. If the pump is mounted on the side of the engine and driven by an accessory shaft, drain the cooling system. Remove the mounting bolts. Remove

the coupling to the pump shaft, and raise the pump from its mounting,
c. Installation.
[1] Front mounted pump. Clean the gasket surface on the engine. Make sure the pump is the correct type and model. Apply a light coat of gasket cement to the pump and engine gasket surfaces and to each side of the gasket. *Editors' Note: I have had good success using the old Permatex™ brand of products.* If the studs were removed from the engine, place them in the pump housing. Hold the pump in position and screw the studs tightly into the engine block. Move the pump against the engine, and install the lock washers and nuts. Tighten them firmly. Install the radiator hose, and fill the cooling system.

[2] Shaft. driven pump. Select a pump of proper type and model, and transfer any accessory fittings from the old pump. Position the pump, and install the attaching bolts. Tighten them firmly. Install the radiator hose, and fill the cooling system.

d. Packing replacement. The packing rings on some pumps may be changed without dismantling the assembly. Unscrew the packing nut from the pump housing, and slide it away from the pump. Then move the packing gland away from the pump. Remove all pieces of the old

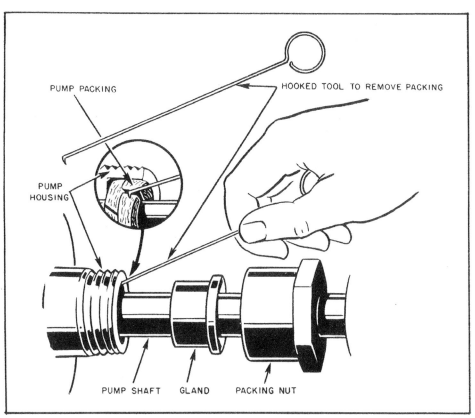

Figure 72. Removing old water-pump packing

packing with a pointed hook tool (fig 72). If there are two packing glands, one nut will unscrew clockwise and the other counterclockwise. The opposing threads are used so that shaft rotation will tend to tighten both nuts. Examine the pump shaft; if it is worn or grooved in the area contacted by the packing, replace the pump. Select new packing rings with an inside diameter that will fit snugly on the shaft. The rings themselves should fit snugly in the packing gland. Use enough rings to fill the packing recess. Place the rings over the shaft, and close the gap in each ring. Force the packing gently into the housing by pushing the gland along the shaft into position. Start the packing nut by hand and tighten it finger tight. Fill the cooling system, start the engine, and tighten the packing nut with a spanner wrench until no water leaks out along the shaft.

99. FAN AND BELT.

a. Fan inspection. Inspect the fan to see that it is firmly fastened to the hub and that the blades are not bent or cracked. Grasp the fan and move it first toward the radiator, then toward the engine. Should there be any play between the fan hub and shaft or between the fan shaft and bearings, replace the assembly.

b. Belt inspection. Crank the engine slowly and inspect the fan belt. Look for broken or frayed material. If the bottom of the "V" in the pulley is bright and shiny, the belt is badly worn. If the fabric is split, the belt adjustment is too tight. If the belt is worn, frayed, or has broken fabric, install a new belt.

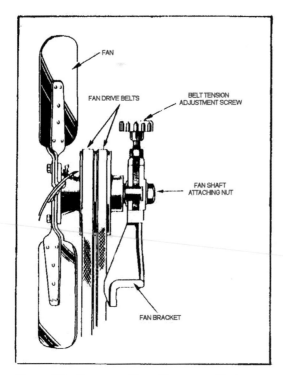

Figure 73. Fan assembly with screw adjustment

c. Fan replacement. If the fan is mounted on the front of the water pump, it is sometimes necessary to remove the pump to replace the fan. If the fan is a separate unit, loosen the lock nut at the rear end of the fan shaft. Loosen the adjustment screw and allow the fan to drop to the lowest position. Then remove the fan belt. Remove the lock nut from the rear of the shaft and the assembly from the bracket.

d. Belt adjustment. Fan belts are generally adjusted either by moving the generator or by positioning the fan assembly in its bracket.

[1] The generator adjustment is made by loosening the generator mounting bolts, then loosening the generator adjusting-arm cap screw. Move the generator either toward or away from the engine until belt tension is correct. Tighten the adjusting arm cap screw, and then tighten the generator mounting bolts,

[2] The fan-assembly adjustment (fig 73) is made by loosening the lock nut at the rear end of the fan shaft. Move the adjustment screw until the fan assembly is positioned to give correct belt tension. Then tighten the lock nut.

[3] Correct belt tension for different vehicles usually varies from 1/2-in. to 1-in. deflection. The correct ten-

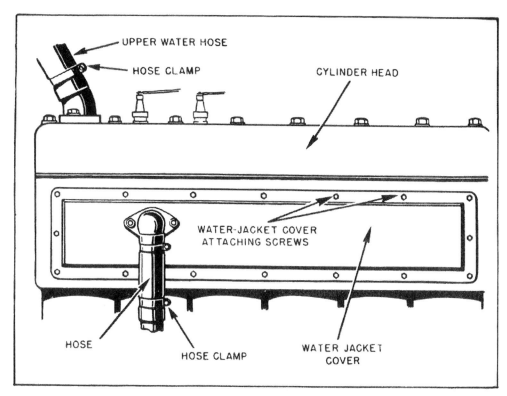

Figure 74. Water-jacket cover

sion can be found in the maintenance manual for each vehicle. If it is not known and is not available, adjust the belt until it can be deflected 3/4-in. at a point midway between the fan and generator drive pulleys.

100. WATER JACKET.
a. Inspection. If a water-jacket cover (fig 74) is attached to the side of the engine, inspect around the edge of the cover for rust streaks or drops of the coolant, both of which will indicate leakage. When leaks are found, tighten the cover attach-

ing screws. If the leakage continues, replace the gasket.

b. Removal. It maybe necessary to remove the oil filter and the radiator or the water-pump hose before the water-jacket cover can be removed. Drain the coolant from the engine, remove the cover screws, and lift the cover from the engine. If the cover sticks, pry it loose gently at two or three points.

c. Replacement. Scrape the gasket material from the surface of the engine and from the cover. If the cover is bent or has burrs on the gasket surface, place it on a flat, metal surface plate or other flat surface (gasket side down) and tap it lightly with a small hammer until it is flat. Apply gasket cement to the cover and one side of the gasket. When the gasket cement is tacky, place the cemented side of the gasket to the cover. Apply cement to the exposed side of the gasket and to the engine. Place the cover in position, and start the cap screws by hand. Then tighten evenly with a wrench. Replace the oil filter and hose connections, and fill the cooling system.

101. THERMOSTAT.

a. Removal. First drain the cooling system. Then remove the upper radiator hose. Remove the nuts from the water-outlet housing, and lift off the housing. Lift the thermostat (fig 75) from lower part of the housing.

b. Inspection. Remove accumulations of rust with steel wool, and see that the seepage hole in the valve is not clogged. Make a visual inspection for bent or distorted frame or damaged bellows. Heat a pan of water to 160°F, using a suitable thermometer to check the temperature; then immerse the thermostat in the water. The valve should begin to open. Remove the thermostat, and heat the water to 185"F.

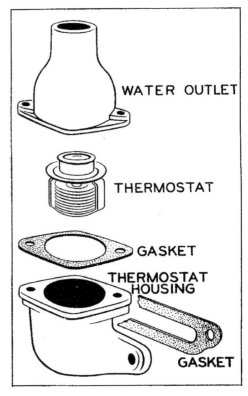

Figure 75. Thermostat assembly

Again immerse the thermostat in the water. The valve should open fully. If the valve does not open properly, do not attempt to repair the thermostat. Replace it with a new unit.

c. Installation. Clean the gasket surfaces of the water-outlet housing and the cylinder-head opening. Place the thermostat in position in the opening of the cylinder head, select a gasket of the proper size. Apply gasket cement to the gasket surfaces of the engine and housing. First slip the gasket and then the housing over the studs. After installing the nuts finger tight, tighten them evenly with a wrench. Over tightening will break or damage the housing, Install the top radiator hose and fill the cooling system.

102. TEMPERATURE GAGE.

a. Inspection. The temperature gage may be one of two types. The thermal type (fig 76) consists of a metal thermometer bulb located in the engine water jacket, a small capillary tube, and a gage in the instrument panel. The electric type consists of a temperature unit in the engine water jacket and a gage on the instrument panel, with a wire between the two and current supplied through the ignition switch. The electric gage will not register unless the switch is on. When the engine is cold, the gage should register "cold." With the cooling system properly filled, start the engine and operate at a fast idle for about 15 minutes. The gage should then register between 140° and 160°F.

b. Replacement.

[1] Thermal type. Drain the cooling system. Remove the nut holding the thermal unit in the engine block and withdraw the bulb. If the bulb sticks because of rust, tap the retainer lightly with a hammer. Remove any clips supporting the capillary tube. Remove the screws that hold the gage unit in the instrument panel and slip the gage away from the panel. Pull the tube and bulb through the hole in the panel, removing the three parts as a single unit. Slip the replacement part through the hole in the panel and fasten the gage mounting screws. Insert the bulb in the engine block, tighten the holding nut, and install any clips supporting the tube. Fill the cooling system.

[2] Electric type. The unit in the engine and the unit on the instrument panel can be replaced individually. To replace the unit on the instrument panel, remove the wires, marking or tagging them for proper identification. Release the mounting screws and remove the gage from the panel. Install the new gage in the same manner. To replace the unit in the engine, first drain the cooling system and remove the wire. Then remove the coupling and lift the unit from the engine.

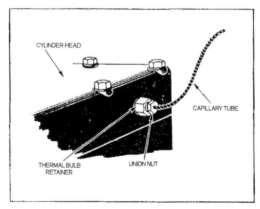

Figure 76. Thermal-bulb temperature-gage connection at engine

INDEX

-rust preventive for 95
-trouble shooting of 92
Corrosion on battery cables 19
Cranking motor
-inspection of 41
-installation of 44
-removal of 43
-switch for 42
-trouble shooting of 41
Crankshaft knock 12

D

Dimmer switch 52
Distributor
-adjustment of 33
-breaker points 27
-condenser 26
-spring tension 30
Distributor cap 24
Distributor rotor 25

E

Electical system 17
Engine
-backfiring 0
-does not start 3
-excessive fuel consumption 10
-excessive oil consumption 11
-lack of power 11
-mechanical knocks 12
-misfiring 9
-operating knocks 11
-overheating 10
-overloaded 11
-trouble shooting of 3
Exhaust manifold 88
Exhaust system 90
Exposed-terminal switch 42

F

Fan 101
Fan belt 101
Filter
-fuel 80
Firing order 32
Flexible hose 85
Fuel consuption, exessive 10
Fuel filter 80
Fuel gage 68
Fuel knock 12
Fuel lines 85
Fuel pump
-electric 77
-mechanical 74
-trouble shooting of 74
Fuel system 61
Fuel tank
Fuse 47

G

Gage
-fuel 68
 temprature 104
Gaskets, test for leaks in 88
Gasoline (see Fuel)
Generator
-inspection of 36
-polarity of 39
-replacement of 40
-trouble shooting of 35
Generator cicuit
-generator 35
-regulator 39
Governor, carburetor 73

1550934

Made in the USA